Billionaire's Habits

Find Out How To Be Part Of The Billionaire Boys Club

By: Tony Giggs

CONGRATULATIONS !!!

You have downloaded " Back to Back: From Childhood to Celebrity". I hope you really enjoy reading this book.

Please, don't forget to leave an honest book review when you get done with reading this awesome book.

I want to dedicate this amazing book to my supporters because i wouldn't be here without ya'll . Thank You So much !!

Table of Contents

Introduction 1

Chapter 1: Where Do I Start? 5

Chapter 2: Wealth Is a State of Mind 13

    The Mentality Effect 17

    Know the Billionaire's Mind 20

    Eliminating Mental Blocks 23

Chapter 3: Billionaire's Lifestyle 1

    Morning Rituals 1

    Right Mindset 9

    Anti-anxiety Routine Billionaire Embrace 11

    Billionaires' Fitness Routine 12

    Billionaires have a Winning Routines 15

Chapter 4: Life Skills Billionaires Master 1

    Making Decisions 1

    Billionaires Prioritize their Activities 6

    Start your Day with Positivity 10

    They Create A Plan of Action 16

    Always Think Big 20

    They have Visions and Ideals 23

    They are Purpose Driven...31

    Have Self-Control 35

    They do not Procrastinate 42

Chapter 5: The Lifestyles of Billionaires: Real Vs. Imagined 1

    The Difference Between Dreaming and Doing................................ 1

Chapter 6: The Relationship between Courage and Wealth 1

Chapter 7: Success Factors 1

    They Understand the Magic of Goals 4

    Dealing with Stressful Situations 12

    Do What They Love 16

Chapter 8: Financial Planning and Debt Management 1

    Billionaire Prioritize their Expenditure 4

    Billionaire have a Debt Management Plan....................................6

    Benefits of Debt Management 10

    Debt Prioritization by Billionaires..12

Chapter 9: Ways Billionaires Redemption from Financial Crisis ... 1

    Focus on What you can Control..6

    Focus on What you Want 10

Chapter 10: Successful vs Average People 1

    Types of People 1

    Breaking from Average 3

    Overcoming Fear of Failure and Ridicule......................................5

Chapter 11: What makes Billionaires Different 1

- Chapter 12: The Economically Productive Household 1
- Chapter 13: Saving Habits of Billionaires 1
  - Cultivating Saving Habit 2
  - Reasons for Saving 4
- Chapter 14: Find a Way to Increase your Income 1
  - Attitude to Possess 4
  - Limit Borrowing 7
- Chapter 15: Roadblocks 1
- Conclusion 1

INTRODUCTION

We all have a lot of dreams; some of us want to become a billionaire and some of us want to find love. Some of us want to have great friendships and we want to live in a great environment that we love and feel comfortable in. Many of us want to succeed at the work we do. One problem with the way many people see their lives, however, is that we see all the different parts as being separate, instead of as one whole. The truth is that all of the different parts are actually connected together as one. This is because they all have to do with how we see ourselves. If you have a negative self image, you are not going to be able to succeed in any aspect of your life. In short, by developing a positive self vision and believing that you can achieve the top, then you can become a billionaire and all other dreams you have for yourself.

This may seem like just another promise that will never be fulfilled. After all, there are a lot of services and tools out there that promise to help you become a billionaire. This makes it so important to choose the best techniques/methods. It begins, perhaps, with positive affirmations. These are little sayings that you can read or listen to, and they will make you feel good about yourself. You will be developing a positive self image as you engage with these affirmations. If you want to get inside the billionaire mind, you have to start with positive thinking.

Is this all it takes to become a billionaire? If you have read this far, then you probably really want to know how to become a billionaire. Well, if you want to take it a step further, then you have to participate in meditation. You are now probably thinking that this sounds like some new age jargon. But the truth is that all meditation requires and is, is concentration. It's all about focusing on yourself and creating the image that you want to see. This is the secret to the billionaire mind. Don't listen to get rich quick schemes. You need to practice self visualization.

In the end, if you want to become a billionaire, you have to focus on yourself and your goals. This is all about two stages. The first is that you have to know who you are. The second is that you have to know who you want to be. By achieving these two stages, you will be able to know how to become a billionaire and accomplish anything else your heart desires. You can find a business coach online who understands this and will help you to inspire yourself to achieve greatness.

What's a billionaire mindset? The answer of the question is simple; it's a basic ingredient that you must possess to become wealthy as well as successful. Thinking, acting and taking decisions like a billionaire is what you may call a billionaire mindset. You don't need to be a billionaire to possess a mindset like it rather it's a necessary element to have in case you wish to become one.

BILLIONAIRE'S HABITS

A billionaire mindset is a great deal different than usual. Here you will learn what attitudes make up the billionaire mindset and in what way it differs from average.

Billionaires think ahead of time; they plan their funds and financial plan for long-term and saves money to make investments for upcoming projects. If you don't have capital now, begin saving and in 6 months or in a year you will possess enough money to begin your own business. 'I am delighted with what I am receiving' won't make you a billionaire even in hundred years.

One important aspect of billionaire mindset is setting goals as well as priorities. Billionaires fix their goals plus are ready to give up their comfort to achieve the goals while average people decline to sacrifice anything. A billionaire makes things turn out for him, an average man wants things happen for him.

Billionaires have faith in their abilities and spend plenty of time to perfect their abilities. They continuously try to learn new stuff and make use of those things to perfect their business. Learning does not end at the time you leave the school rather real education takes place after the school.

Billionaires spend some time for doing things they prefer best. If you're not enjoying your life you will not be able to devote yourself in achieving your goals.

Most individuals do not have a clean idea about what they actually desire. They leap forward with uncertainty while a billionaire knows precisely the things that he wishes and can take steps and plan his moves with an unmistakable view in mind.

Waiting for opportunities is not what billionaires do, they create opportunities for themselves. Billionaires think big but they are aware that initially it's good to start small and they do not shy away from challenges.

Billionaires will take their chances to earn money. If they fail they don't lose their attitude. They realize the fact that no one can be successful all the time. Try persistently is what the billionaire mindset tells you to do. average men do quite the opposite of this. They are scared of losing their money and remain with the exact same earning for the whole life.

With the same qualifications as yours, many people have had success and gained plenty of money in their life. Haven't you questioned if that individual was you! Well, stop questioning and try to learn from them. And begin with changing your mindset because it is the first move in the way to become one of them.

Thank you for choosing to read this book. I believe it will be essential and answer your questions, therefore read on.

CHAPTER 1

WHERE DO I START?

A billionaire mindset does not just happen for most. Becoming a billionaire isn't about snapping your fingers and poof, you have it. Bank accounts don't just fill because we want them to. There are several traits and steps that must be taken. Here are a few of the traits you need to live your dream with money in your pocket.

A Vision

Having a Billionaire mindset starts with a vision. A billionaire has a creative vision with a positive attitude. This means that not only do billionaires have big dreams, but they truly believe that their dreams will come true and they will do anything they need to to see that dream come true. You are what your thoughts are. Setting a large goal for yourself and seeing it through to fruition is a huge start towards dollars in the pocket.

Thinking Differently

Billionaires don't just think differently about money, but they think differently about everything. While most are spending time on menial, unproductive tasks, a person with a billionaire mindset is spending brain power on ways to create their path. Independent thinking doesn't necessarily mean doing the opposite of everyone else; it means finding the courage to follow your dreams even if they don't always conform to everyone else's thinking. Billionaires find ways for money to work for them; they don't chase money. For example, if your dreams are to become a world renowned author, then focus you thinking on ways to do that.

Having Skills

Billionaires never quit learning new skills. They read, they learn and constantly go with the times. Instead of hanging around with people who have the same skill level as they do, they normally will hang around and choose colleagues who offer a supplement to their weaker skills. So to learn new skills, you can use training or mentors to strengthen your skills. Those with a billionaire mindset will normally choose a mentor that is in a position that they strive to be in. For example, if someone is striving to be a billionaire, they don't hang out or use mentors that aren't making a million dollars already. They don't hang out with people with a job mentality.

Have Passion

The billionaire mindset also has a lot to do with passion. To billionaires, money is just a by-product of something that they like to do very much. You have to have a true passion for what you are doing to incorporate it into every part of your life. The statistic of finding your true passion isn't until approximately age 45 and achieving the million dollars, or more usually isn't statistically until age 54. If you want to be a billionaire, start doing things that makes your heart sing and stop doing things that you do not love. If you are not sure what that is, start trying new things until you find the right fit for you!

Being a Salesman

Those with a billionaire mindset also know that salesmanship is one of the best skills they can learn. Billionaires constantly are presenting their ideas and persuading other people to buy into their visions. That is all sales is; persuasion and getting people to buy in. A good salesperson has a tough diamond skin that is oblivious to naysayers and critical people. Billionaires also have great interpersonal skills and can socialize well. It starts with being able to sell yourself so polish and practice this skill every single day on someone, anyone. It not only helps you get better at the skill of sales but also helps you build a larger, more loyal network of people.

Smart Investing and Living Within Your Means

When you are a billionaire, spending a few hundred bucks on a shopping trip seems like no big deal and it isn't. But while you are trying to get there, you need to mind your dollars and cents. Someone with a billionaire mindset will make sure they are spending smart and spending on the right things. The right things to invest in are yourself, your education you need for your idea, and it never hurts to budget. Would you rather go without that extra latte for a few years if you knew that you could have everything your heart desires?? Of course, you would!

Unfortunately, becoming a billionaire doesn't come at the drop of the hat and is a risk, to say the least, but the advantages far outweigh the disadvantages. With some confidence, the ability to make a strong decision put those new skills to the test and to never let that vision out of your site (not even for a minute); you can have whatever you want in life and your pocket!

Well, creating a billionaire mindset is pivotal to your success in business especially in network marketing. This maybe why you are struggling with no success in your business and wondering why. Even if you have the best business opportunity, the best compensation plan, or even the best marketing system, not changing your mindset will have you spinning in circles and not achieving any success. So here are three pivotal pillars to help you in creating a billionaire mindset. They are education, company, and activity.

Education

What do you put into your brain daily? In other to create a billionaire mindset you have to increase your knowledge and the only way of doing this is by educating yourself. There are no shortcuts! You have to invest in educating yourself on the industry of network marketing as this is the only way you will understand what the business is about. There are a variety of books out there on the industry and mindset some are Think and Grow Rich by

Napoleon Hill, Rich Dad Poor Dad by Robert Kiyosaki, How to Win Friends and Influence People by Dale Carnegie and a host more!

Another way of acquiring information is by attending live events and training. This can be powerful as you do not just get the training you also build relationships with fellow like-minded individuals. Education is critical because we are all a product of what we believe and we tend to believe what we know. So if what you know is not getting you closer to creating a billionaire mindset then I guess you have to improve that by learning new material. You have to know exactly where you want to be and what your goals you want to achieve. In network marketing, you have to believe that you are going to be successful in whatever you are doing.

You must avoid negative thoughts and be positive at all times, thoughts or comments like "I will try" or "I hope this works" automatically sets your brain up for failure. You should be confident that your business will succeed because you will be responsible for making it a success. You are the only one that has the power to make your life the way you want it, and it can be done only if you educate yourself the right way.

Company

A saying goes, "tell me your friends and I will tell you who you are." This rings true for the most part. In creating a billionaire mindset, you have to be in the company of the people you would like to be like. I am not saying to dump your friends/family and make new ones. However, you have to truly evaluate those that encourage you in what you are doing and those that try to pull you down as a result of their lack of understanding. Answer this,"Are you living for your friends and family or you?" For you, I hope!

You should keep your relationships, but focus on associating yourself with the people you want to be like, learn from them, and duplicate their success. A great place to meet people is in training seminars as I mentioned above. Life long relationships are built this way. Time is the most important asset in the world and if you waste it associating primarily with the wrong people then creating a billionaire mindset for yourself will never be realized.

Activity

What actions do you take on a daily basis in creating that billionaire mindset? Watch TV? Surf the internet? To create a billionaire mindset, you need to get laser focused on taking action. You have to develop a plan, goal or a systematic approach to whatever you set out to do. You have to turn your education into action and be consistent with it. In business, the success that everyone wants is not a mystery, but just having the mindset of doing the things that others won't do.

I have often heard that working paycheck to paycheck will never make one a billionaire; this is not consistent in creating a billionaire mindset. According to the late Jim Rohn, "in other to make a fortune you have to make profits" So if you are in this situation, you have thought of doing something else or adding to what you are doing now. You would have to learn how to shift from the employee mentality to the entrepreneur mentality. Yes, granted this is a long potentially difficult process, however, if you do not start it, it will never be done.

Sounds radical? Yes, it is, but if you can wrap the mind around this concept, then you can slowly start changing how you think and start learning new skills. You have to decide to change what you are doing if it is not getting you to creating a billionaire mindset of success.

So there you have it, creating a billionaire mindset is crucial to your success in business. Remember that this is a process. There has to be a mental shift in how you think for your mindset to change.

CHAPTER 2

WEALTH IS A STATE OF MIND

If you want to be wealthy and to keep the wealth you have, you need to take care of one thing above all else, that is your mind. Your mind must be prepared for the wealth that is coming if you are truly going to receive it and be able to keep it. The following three reasons should give you clarity on why preparing yourself mentally is the most important thing you can do for gaining and keeping wealth.

The road is tough and can only be survived if you are mentally tough

The first reason you need to prepare yourself mentally is that the road to wealth is tough. That is just the way it is. You are going to be tested along the way, faced with challenges and difficulties that would make the average person stop and give in.

Want proof, look around you, how many people that you know are wealthy? Everyone has the capability to be wealthy, there is no unique gene for wealth, but only a few actually achieve it. These people achieve it because they had the mental strength and toughness to make sure they did what they needed to do to achieve what they wanted. Only mental strength and preparation will get you through to the goal of wealth.

You mental, financial blueprint will decide your level of success

The second reason you need to prepare for wealth mentally is that ultimately your level of financial success is ultimately determined by where your mental, financial thermostat rests. This mental, financial thermostat is the level of wealth you are mentally prepared to have.

Most people have a thermostat set for just getting by or comfortable. Some have a thermostat at below their income so they are perpetually in debt and it always seems to get worse. Very few people have their thermostat set for wealthy and abundance.

It doesn't matter if you come into a large sum of money or not, you will eventually end up back at the level your thermostat is originally set for. Why do you think the majority of lottery winners eventually end up back where they were, their thermostats were not set to handle the new wealth. So you need to work on your mental, financial thermostat if you want to be able to have and keep the wealth coming your way.

You mind your reality

The third and final reason you need to prepare yourself mentally are that your mind creates your reality. If your mind is not in the right place, your reality will not end up I the right place. There is no way around this fact, what we believe we shall see.

There is a simple equation that explains how this works. T-F-A=R. This is simply the basic rule of life: your thoughts become your feelings, which become your actions, which equal your results. If you are not actively working on your mental thoughts, then the rest will not fall into place. You have to get your mental house for everything else to work out.

Hopefully, these three reasons help you to see why you need to working on preparing yourself mentally if you want to be wealthy. Without a strong mental foundation the wealth with not arrive or stay. So get to work on developing your mental focus and clarity.

Think it, and it will come. It is the heart of the law of attraction that made The Secret and other books bestsellers. Many readers try to incorporate warm, fuzzy thoughts into their daily routine, only to be disappointed when the wealth beyond reason they dreamed of just doesn't find them.

The truth? Alone, all the sunniest, fuzziest thoughts in the world can't create a wealth mentality. Here are the wealth secrets you need to know about:

Wealth Secret #1 - Focus, Daniel-san

It is not just about taking the time to focus; creating wealth beyond reason involves what you focus on as well. Maybe you're stuck in a cruddy job, working cruddier hours, and lorded over by the cruddiest of bosses. If your inner dialogue consists of "I hate my job. I hate my boss. I hate my co-workers" then your energy is consumed by negative emotions.

Create a wealth mentality by banishing those blue thoughts from your mind and cultivating the positive: "I have the skills and talent to create wealth beyond reason" or "I attract wealth like a magnet attracts nails." The wealth secret that will help you achieve your money goals is to generate positive emotions, the kind that attracts all the good things the universe has to offer

Wealth Secret #2 - We all need somebody to lean on

Creating a wealth mentality can be hard, especially if friends and family aren't as supportive as they need to be. That's why you need a good support system. Whether it's a like-minded friend who's believed in the law of attraction for years or a professional support team that offers expertise through a book or seminar, getting the right motivation can be an important step in building wealth beyond reason.

Remember to make those resources a part of your daily routine. If you've read The Secret once, that's fine and dandy, but you might need the constant reinforcement that comes from expertly written affirmations or a professional wealth mentality consultant.

Wealth Secret #3 - Back to life, back to reality

It is fine to keep a journal full of affirmations, after all, it can take a while rid your mind of the negative recordings you've accumulated over a lifetime. Building wealth beyond reason, however, is more than just thinking happy thoughts-you've got to take those thoughts and turn them into reality. That means when an opportunity comes, even if it's in a form you weren't expecting, you need to grab it.

It is true that the happy thoughts that attract wealth beyond reason aren't enough. By surrounding yourself with expert information and concrete actions, you can create the wealth mentality that will carry you into the lifestyle you deserve.

The Mentality Effect

You want to find out how billionaires become billionaires so you can become one yourself. Your reasons for pursuing this dream may be you want significant wealth, or to have a family lifestyle that wealth can give you, it may be for peace of mind that comes from financial freedom. Whatever the reasons, you need to decide why you want this money as this is what will drive and motivate you to turn your dream into reality.

Becoming a billionaire may sound very far away to you, but it can only be achieved if you allow yourself to follow certain steps. These steps have no time limit on them, therefore, you can become as rich as quick as you want to be. If you consistently apply the lessons below you will see your wealth start to increase.

Here are the truths you need to become the billionaire you want to be:

Billionaire mindset

Your mindset will have to change, you have to believe that you can become a billionaire and even more importantly that you deserve to be a billionaire, don't undervalue yourself. You have to be determined to work hard and commit to what you believe will make you succeed. It is that motivation and mindset which enables all those billionaires to persevere.

Consider what you are doing now

You will have to face the fact that there is a very small chance that you will make money working for somebody else. Working for an employer only makes them richer not you. So to become a billionaire, the vast majority of people will have to start working for themselves. You will have to be prepared to step out of your comfort zone and explore the world of entrepreneurs.

Find a helpful billionaire

There is not much you can learn from someone about making a lot of money if they only make a small amount for themselves. Find a billionaire mentor who is willing to show you the ropes, someone you can learn the essentials from. Don't expect them to do the work for you but they will give you lots of tips and ideas that will show you how to become and remain a success.

This way you can implement their actions into your plan.

Start investing instead of spending

Once you start to make money, you may be tempted to spend on luxurious and stylish items. This is not a problem as long as it is balanced. However, saving is important as earning and is a discipline that you will need to learn. So instead of buying items that you do not need invest in shares or stocks or art. The point is to put your money into assets that will make you wealthier rather than possessions that only show that you are wealthy but in the long term are just a drain on your cash. OK, you may not be able to do this right away, but you now understand the concept. This is what billionaires do to earn extra money.

Have more than one income

Billionaires do something that ordinary people rarely do. They have multiple sources of income. Beginning to invest can generate extra income, but there are also different ways in which you can do this too. Once you begin to make the income, you have targeted at achieving, you will soon find that other opportunities present themselves, you should then develop another business, so it begins to earn you more money. As you generate some revenue streams, you become less reliant on any one and therefore protect your lifestyle.

You will stand in your way

The sooner you realize that the only person that will stop you achieving is yourself, the sooner you will be able to address this when it begins to happen. When you start to become successful, do not begin to second guess yourself. But follow through on your plan. You will need to stay focused on your goals so remove any fears or negativity.

Becoming a billionaire is not easy and pursuing it will be difficult. Believe in yourself and begin to formulate an action plan, with all your goals and targets and then take one step at a time. Your effort will reap the rewards, as long as you act on what you want and evaluate how you are doing and continue to follow these truths on how billionaires become billionaires.

Know the Billionaire's Mind

You may find that they have been working so hard for and don't have any money left over at the end of the month to pay your bills. Possibly you do not have money put away for luxuries like going on a Caribbean cruise or having a luxurious vacation in the Seychelles. Are you still driving around in your old banger of a car while all the time someone else is showing of their latest gleaming car to add to their collection?

What is it that she/he has that you don't? Are they just luckier than you are? Probably, the big difference between you and that person is that they have cultivated a billionaire mindset.

You are probably thinking to yourself right now, "what is a billionaire mindset?" Well you see, your mind is very powerful. But do you know that your subconscious mind is even more powerful? The subconscious mind is a compilation of all the things you have experienced since you were young. Your subconscious mind acts as a "storehouse" of everything you have gone through in your life. These things affect the way you think and the way you do things.

You may not be aware of it, but there are things there in your mind that dictate your every action which are far different from what you consciously think about. So if you have, at some point in your life, found that a more simplistic lifestyle is far better than a financially well-off lifestyle, then you may have a challenge trying to acquire wealth. If you have experienced the acquisition of money as being not a good thing, then you may have a difficulty getting your first million.

Achieving a billionaire mind takes a lot of work and involves the undoing of limiting that you have acquired over the years. It can be done, but you will need to find the right tools to help you. Once you start to think in a positive way about the acquisition of money, then it will become a whole lot easier to acquire it. In fact, you may find that out of the blue money is indeed coming your way.

Having a billionaire's mindset is in no way steeped in mystery. It is achievable to every human being if they want to achieve a rich lifestyle. What you think about is what you will start to see showing up in your life. We are a mirror of the world, so if we start to think and act positively towards the accomplishment of acquiring wealth, then this will start to show up in your life. It may not be very noticeable at first, but life has a funny way of giving us everyday signs, and if we are "conscious" of these signs and act on them, then you will start to see the end results which can be lucrative.

We all have a lot of dreams; some of us want to become a billionaire and some of us want to find love. Some of us want to have great friendships, and we want to live in a great environment that we love and feel comfortable in. Many of us want to succeed at work we do. One problem with the way many people see their lives, however, is that we see all the different parts of being separate, instead of as one whole. The truth is that all of the different parts are connected together as one. This is because they all have to do with how we see ourselves. If you have a negative self-image, you are not going to be able to succeed in any aspect of your life. In short, by developing a positive self-vision and believing that you can achieve the top, then you can become a billionaire and all other dreams you have for yourself.

This may seem like just another promise that will never be fulfilled. After all, there are a lot of services and tools out there that promise to help you become a billionaire. This makes it so important to choose the best techniques/methods. It begins, perhaps, with positive affirmations. These are little sayings that you can read or listen to, and they will make you feel good about yourself. You will be developing a positive self-image as you engage with these affirmations. If you want to get inside the billionaire mind, you have to start with positive thinking.

Is this all it takes to become a billionaire? If you have read this far, then you probably really want to know how to become a billionaire. Well, if you want to take it a step further, then you have to participate in meditation. You are now probably thinking that this sounds like some new age jargon. But the truth is that all meditation requires and is, is concentration. It's all about focusing on yourself and creating the image that you want to see. This is the secret to the billionaire mind. Don't listen to get rich quick schemes. You need to practice self-visualization.

In the end, if you want to become a billionaire, you have to focus on yourself and your goals. This is all about two stages. The first is that you have to know who you are. The second is that you have to know who you want to be. By achieving these two stages, you will be able to know how to become a billionaire and accomplish anything else your heart desires. You can find a business coach online who understands this and will help you to inspire yourself to achieve greatness.

Eliminating Mental Blocks

Mental blocks come in many forms. You don't have to sit in front of a computer unable to type. You may want to write but never find the time. You find excuse after excuse to avoid writing. Procrastination becomes your second name. Excuses range from shopping, taking care of the kids, meeting friends, talking on the telephone, watching TV soaps, reading too much, constantly redecorating the house, lingering over meals and being lost in thought. None of these activities are bad. It's just that most of them could be reduced, eliminated or controlled freeing up time to write.

If you just can't seem to eliminate any of your time-consuming activities, this may be evidence of a mental block that isn't immediately obvious. If you believe that may be the case here is an Imagery exercise that might help you.

Imagery Exercise to Stop Wasting Time

If watching too much television or reading too much or just being lazy seems to be taking time from your wish to write, try this Imagery. Imagine that you are sitting watching TV when the television set explodes casting debris all over you and a hideous monster comes out of the debris and pounces on you. You are scared beyond belief. Even if you don't feel scared, pretend. Act the role. You want to influence your mind to make television less palatable.

Suddenly you awaken to the fully accepted realization that you can overcome this monstrous beast and with a great show of strength you grasp it in your powerful hands and throw it at you or you break its neck and kill it. Exclaim in a loud and committed voice that you will never watch TV excessively again. It will never stop you from being a highly creative person. Exult in your newfound power and know you will become a highly creative person.

If you prefer a less negative Imagery exercise, imagine that you are watching the TV and find that you can't concentrate. You become sleepy and can't fully awaken. You feel that the TV controls you. You then raise your arm, point to the TV and command that it goes off. You get up, feeling powerful and happy that you have broken the tie to the TV. Your affirmation might be simply, "I'll never excessively watch soaps or television again."

Always keep in mind that when you use Imagery, you put strong feelings into it and you believe in the power of your mind to transform you. Be persistent! No matter how many days or weeks you practice the Imagery, be patient and you will find a change in your behavior. If you encounter resistance to doing the Imagery remember that you are doing them to change thinking and behavior. Your mind knows the intent, and it works because you want it to work. The exercise depends on your mindset, your belief in the process and the belief in yourself. Keep it up. You will be successful.

You can rapidly and effectively expand your creative life by following the methods and exercises described in "Awakening Your Creativity." In this book, you will find the primary tools to change your life in ways that will excite and delight you. You can become creative.

Niche business ideas are declining in America for the first time. This is in line with the latest research by the University of California that overall American creativity is declining. The gap between the U.S and the rest of the world is narrowing by staggering amounts.

Many experts, including Sir Ken Robinson, feel it's because we're slowly educating people out of their creativity. "Our schools have been teaching us to be good workers, rather than creative thinkers," says the creativity expert.

In fact, because of our low priority to teach and encourage creative thinking in our educational system many people develop mental blocks. These mental blocks diminish, squelch and limit the creativity in most of us.

The big challenge is finding ways to restore our natural creativity, imagination and innovative thinking - schools continue to educate out of most of us.

Here's The Top 3 Mental Blocks To Getting More Profitable Ideas for Your Business.

Mental Block #1
Giving Up on Illogical Ideas Too Soon

Did you know some of history's greatest ideas started out as illogical? Fortunately, the creators never let that stop them. For example, everything from the light bulb and jet plane - to the personal computer and smartphone were first all illogical ideas.

Yes, the ideas started out as illogical dreams of the creator - but through persistent research and adjustments, they worked their way to a logical result. The bar of logic is always moving - and continues to move faster in this high tech/information age.

What's was illogical or even said to be impossible just a few years ago is the reality now. From cars that drive themselves to the commercial value of rap music and everything in between. Who would have thought?

So, don't be afraid to start with an illogical idea. Because if you have one you're in good company. That's what some of our country's greatest innovators such as Thomas Edison, Steve Jobs Bill Gates, and others started with.

Mental Block# 2
Looking At Problems As Bad Instead of As Opportunities

With problems all around us, the first reaction of most people is to ignore, run or even deny them. But idea-minded people see problems as opportunities instead of obstacles. In fact, the only reason something is bought or sold is that the buyer is trying to solve a problem.

Whatever motivates your customer or prospect to buy from you instead of a competitor is because you solve more of a higher priority problem.

So, don't let this mental block stop you. Don't run from problems... run to them. Why? Because that's where your next profitable idea is hidden.

Yes, most people constantly miss golden opportunities each day, because they often come disguised as problems. Now you know!

Listen to your market, to your customers, to your prospects seek out any problems they're having. This is one simple action that could lead you to bigger profits, increased sales, and more repeat business.

Mental Block #3
Underestimating The Power of a Small Idea

Big ideas often steal the show when it comes to idea creation. Everyone is looking for the big idea that revolutionizes an industry.

But did you realize how many small ideas have revolutionized industries as well?

In fact, many small ideas have stood the test of time better than the so-called big ideas. For example, the paper clip, the toothpick, or the nail file, to name a few.

In my opinion, small ideas don't get close to enough credit or respect for their contributions. People often overlook small ideas because of ignorance to their importance in the creative process.

Yes, small ideas can be the beginning of a big idea. But a small idea in itself has been known to boost sales, reignite profits and even save a business from bankruptcy. So, never underestimate the power of a small idea. The screw was a small idea, but I dare you or anyone to fly in a plane that didn't have one.

By simply being aware of these 3 mental blocks, you'll have all the tools you'll need to start overcoming them. Awareness and persistent actions are the best way you can push back against the obstacles to getting more profitable ideas.

CHAPTER 3

BILLIONAIRE'S LIFESTYLE

Morning Rituals

Take a minute to imagine how much more productive you would be if you were able to wake up just an hour or two earlier in the morning. They'd be nothing and nobody to distract you from getting on with whatever you want! The only things stopping you are the sleeping habits that you've built up over the years. You may have tried in the past to reverse these habits but without the proper techniques that it's very hard to do. Fortunately, I'm going to share with you five tips that will make waking up early every morning a piece of cake!

1. Go to sleep earlier! This is perhaps the most important of these tips. Realistically you can't expect to go to sleep at 1 am and then be able to wake up as fresh as a daisy at 5 am. A good rule of thumb is to aim for seven hours sleep. That means that if you want to wake up at 5 am, you should be going to sleep at 10 pm.

2. Build a routine. The human mind responds well to routine and quickly forms routine into a habit. In the example above I said that you should be asleep by 10pm, well that means you should also be in bed by 9:30 pm at the latest. Even before then though you have an opportunity to prepare your mind and body for sleep. A good routine would be to finish all chores and tasks by 8 pm and then to start unwinding by perhaps taking a bath and the reading a book. Try doing this for a few days, and you will soon find that you start to become sleepy as soon as you pick up your book as your mind knows it is soon time to fall asleep according to the routine you have been following.

3. Set your alarm and place it at the other end of the room! The snooze button will probably be your worst enemy in your efforts to wake up earlier. That is why you should set for alarm for the exact time you want to wake up (don't try and trick yourself by setting it early and then snoozing for thirty minutes) and put it somewhere where you'll have to get up to turn it off. You might even want to set up two or three alarms in this manner!

4. Drink a drink. After you've been sleeping for seven hours, your body will be dehydrated. That is why it's a good idea to put a glass of water by your bed. As soon as you wake up (or turn off those alarms!) drink the full glass of water. This will hydrate and energize your body, making you feel a lot more awake and less likely to hop back into bed.

5. Program your mind. This may sound a tricky task since you're not a robot or computer, but you can program your

mind with a technique known as hypnosis. Hypnosis speaks to the part of your mind which holds your habits and routines which are why it's so effective for people looking to quit smoking or lose weight. The same can also be said of waking up early. You can find hypnosis MP3s on the subject of waking up early, and they do work!

Chaos is what is usually experienced by most parents during most mornings, especially on weekdays. Most parents get stressed up as they try to prepare their families for the day ahead, this would be a thing of the past if most parents learn how to lay strategies for the next day at the eve of that day.

Parents can prepare for the next morning by organizing oneself the previous evening. Duties that do not necessarily need to be performed early in the morning can be performed at night before going to sleep. Washing the dishes that have been used at supper time does not necessarily need to be washed in the morning if they can be washed at night.

Preparation of breakfast early can also be a way of saving time. This can be done by stocking ready cooked light foods low in calories and fat such as cornflakes. This will assist in the preparation of breakfast the next morning.

Parents should also try not to engage in activities that may distract the children's attention as they prepare for school, activities such as watching television tend to capture the children's attention as they prepare to make them to consume a lot of time performing a specific chore.

Parents should try to ensure that they are in control of everything that is being done early in the morning; this will minimize cases of students engaging in activities that will eat up most of the time required for preparation for school.

For the personal belongings of the children such as the shoes, school uniform and the books, parents should try as much as they can to partition their room so that each child can have a selected place where they can place their personal belongings. These will make it easy for the children to retrieve them the following morning as they prepare for school.

This can be done by parents setting up lockers or drawers where each child can place his/her personal effects required for the school, this tends to make preparation easy for the children and it also assists you as a parent to locate some of the effects a specific child might be missing

After performing this parent need to lighten up before leaving for work so as to have a nice day.

Motivation is a funny thing; it takes many different forms; sometimes you may be motivated to do something out of boredom, where other times you may want to do something for someone else, or to benefit yourself.

There are a few different types of motivation to be aware of. There are two categories these motivators will fit under: one, positive motivators and two, negative motivators.

Motivation spurred from boredom is a bad source to draw your energy from. If you have to be completely devoid of action and stuck in a tedious and wearisome state before you feel the need to do something, I would guess that you do not have a very strong goal.

If, however, you do have a goal and you still find yourself in bleak and utter boredom, ask yourself what it is that you are avoiding, or why it is that you are not going for your goal? If you say, it is because there is nothing you can do at present... I'd call you a liar.

There is always something you can do, even if it's just going to bed early to wake up in the morning. Even that is better than procrastinating everything all together and just wasting time and energy.

To keep motivated you will want to let yourself be reminded. This can be as simple as an association to creative little notes posted on the mirrors and dressers, and maybe the fridge.

One big thing with people not being motivated is that they are too scared they will fail. There is something worse than losing, and that is never trying.

Many people avoid conversations or block them out with doublethink, which is a bizarre thing to do. We have all done it, where we have not been honest with ourselves and either ignored something that was affecting us, or speaking or acting contrary to something we knew.

Why do we do this? This could be for a lot of reasons.

It could be the lack of self-esteem, you do not trust yourself, or you are scared to show who you are to people around you. Whatever the case may be you cannot live with two thoughts or ideas set against each other.

One day when you are not expecting it, one of the ideas is going to collapse under the pressure. What will be left of you then... whatever wasn't invested in the broken paradigm?

You have to be bold enough to try what it is you want. There is you before there is anyone else, so do all you can do, and be all you can be.

You might notice this but there are some days that we feel excited about and as the day goes on, you feel your energy slowly decline. You begin to feel afternoon slumps which make it harder to work when you are pressing for a deadline. Take time off to read the following to see what you can do to make things better for you at work.

So, the very first thing we do is to grab a cup of coffee when we feel the afternoon slump, right? But, that might not be the best advice you can get. It all starts on your lifestyle then your diet. There should be some form of modification to help you avoid afternoon slumps.

An eight-hour sleep can do good for your body. The moment your head lies on the pillow and you get to have a good night's sleep, your body regains its normal pace and it helps you revitalize your energy level for the next day.

Diet is a crucial factor when it comes to rest and sleep. There are certain foods that help you sleep a lot faster and better and there are others that will make sleeping a tedious process. Coffee and other caffeinated drinks should be avoided by late afternoon and should be replaced with milk.

Fruits and vegetables are a great way to help you sustain your energy for the rest of the day. Munch on an apple in the morning rather than a cup of coffee and while you are working, have a pouch of nuts under your desk to help your brain work faster.

Doing cardio workouts and aerobics help regulates blood circulation enabling all the nutrients that you eat to certain parts of the body that need it. Plus, exercise also flushes out toxins through sweat and urine.

Do not forget to make room for rests. Do an afternoon nap or get yourself off from your office seat and talk to your co-workers as well. It might spark up a good idea for your project, or you can always take the time to clear your mind from work.

When you have tried these things and still you have problems with how you go to work and how you still feel tired the morning after, it is a time that you talk to your doctor.

What morning routines do you have? After having had a good night's sleep, how we run our morning is important to how our day goes.

How can you make a mediocre morning become a great morning? Well, for starters, you need to get up at a sensible time, early in the morning.

Some people follow this routine with great success. First, they get out of bed and open several windows in the house to let the house get some fresh air for them to breathe. Next, they brush their teeth, wash there face, and drink a couple of glasses of water.

Many people find that exercising is a great help to their mood, but they are doing more than just getting their mood up. They are also getting their body in shape. Some people may go for a quick morning walk or jog, while others may do yoga and meditate.

After your exercise routine, it would probably be a good idea to take a bath or shower. Warm water will help you to feel the most relaxed and refreshed.

Make sure you eat a healthy breakfast before your morning is too far gone. Proper nutrition will go a long way to making you feel better and be at your best.

Those morning chores always seem to get you down? Try listening to your favorite music while doing them to put you in a better frame of mind. Or, read a book or newspaper a few minutes before starting your chores, so you have something constructive to think about.

Before you leave the house or start your work, spend a few minutes making a list of things you would like to accomplish before the day is done. Also, spend sufficient time on your looks. If you look good, it will help lift your spirits. Try to look cheerful. If you look cheerful, most people will respond in kind, and that will make your day easier.

At the end of the day, take account of everything you have done. Did things work good or bad? Also, prepare for tomorrow by tidying up your house, ironing your clothes, and going to bed at a decent time. This will help you avoid having a stressful day tomorrow. These are just a few different ways you can start your morning.

Right Mindset

There are many ways to develop the right mindset for personal growth, and you as an individual have to choose the ones that are going to work for you. Personal growth takes dedication and self-discipline, and if you don't commit to changing your mindset and working towards change on a daily basis, you can forget to see any major achievements and changes in your personal growth.

To start the process off, it is always best to find yourself a hero. Pick somebody that has done well in his or her own life and used them as an example of what you need to work towards. Do what you have to, short of stalking them, to pick that person's brain. Follow them on Twitter and become a Facebook fan if you have to. Do what you can to see how they live, plan, set goals and try to follow their examples. See if you can find somebody who can coach you, as this is the best way to learn from example.

Changing your mindset also involves getting rid of bad habits and thought patterns. There are many excellent books available on this topic. Keep a mindset book at your bedside, and commit to reading it for at least twenty minutes each day. Once you have finished it, read it again so that all the information can sink in and you will start thinking more about implementing it into your daily lives.

Personal growth is a daily exercise, and you will need to find some time each day to reflect on your goals and your future. The best way to do this is to close your eyes and picture in detail how you would like your future to be. Picture what you will be doing the day your reach your next goal, and picture it in as much detail as you can.

Personal growth involves changing all those negative thoughts into positive ones. It is a difficult thing to do, and you will need to be very aware of what you are thinking. In the beginning, this will be the hardest part of your personal growth, and if you fail at something, you will need to look at that failure positively and learn from the experience.

Setting targets and goals is a must do, and you need to keep a list of your goals where you can see them so that they are never far from your mind. It is also not enough to just set goals, you also need to plan just how you are going to achieve your goals, and steps must take on a daily basis to shift you closer to those goals.

Anti-anxiety Routine Billionaire Embrace

Do you suffer from feelings of unease? Have they lasted a lot longer than they usually do, and do they seem to come out of nowhere? If so you may be suffering from problematic anxiety or anxiety disorder. Many times, anxiety disorder happens when there is an underlying mental health condition like depression already present. If a person has a lot of anxiety that interferes with their daily life and makes everyday routines hard, it is a problem.

Sometimes anxiety can even cause physical symptoms. You may experience such troubles as diarrhea, chest pain, heart palpitations, and even shaking due to anxiety disorder. You need to be seen by your doctor if you have any of those symptoms, or if you feel you have anxiety. Your doctor can tell you how to treat your condition so that you don't get worse. Here are some of the treatments that are available for anxiety:

Daily exercise can greatly reduce your anxiety. It does not have to be strenuous exercise. Even just thirty minutes of light jogging or walking in the mornings can provide some relief and eventually lead to your anxiety resolving.

Your doctor may also prescribe medication. Sometimes patients are given anti-anxiety medications, other times antidepressants may be used. The goal is to help you reduce and eventually eliminate the anxious feelings. Remember always to take the medication you are given as prescribed and in the correct dosage.

Deep breathing exercises will help you feel calmer. You can balance and relax your mind and body by taking deep breaths. Even better, this will increase the level of oxygen in your body and help resolve any chemical imbalances.

If you make it a point to do these things each day, your anxiety will dwindle and eventually disappear. There is no reason why you should continue to suffer the misery of crippling anxiety when it is unnecessary.

Billionaires' Fitness Routine

We live in a fast-paced world, where we often find it challenging to take out quality time for ourselves. This is one of the main reasons why a majority of the population has a hard time trying to fit in exercise into their daily routines. On the flip side, people who manage to exercise early in the morning can enjoy countless benefits that shape and discipline their health and daily routines effectively.

Here's why morning workouts are a fantastic way to kick-start your day.

A Morning Workout Is a Better Workout

Normally, your body is conditioned to perform at its best around mid-afternoon. However, if you schedule your workouts during that time, "life" is bound to happen. There will always be too much work, or a rush assignment getting in the way of your workout. Making exercise a regular part of your early morning routines, helps you maintain a regular regime. Studies even reveal that once the human body adjusts to the morning routine, it may even outperform the afternoon performance.

There's Plenty Time for Other Things

Exercise is important, but there are other important things as well - things like family! When you put off your exercise routine for later, you have to trade-off quality time you could spend with family for exercising. Once you get done with your exercise routine early in the morning, you can do whatever you want without your mind being crowded with the thought of having missed out on your workout.

You End Up Burning More Fat

You may have come across a series of pros and cons of working out on an empty stomach. However, according to a 2013 study, you can burn up to 20% more body fat through early morning exercises.

It Gives Your Metabolism a Boost

Whether you're undertaking weight loss exercises, or concentrating on aerobic exercise training, the working out will boost your metabolism. The extent to which the metabolic rate improves depends on the type of physical activity you choose, and your physical fitness level. Ceteris paribus, a morning workout is comparatively more effective on the metabolism owing to the EPOC (post-exercise oxygen consumption) - the phenomenon that allows you to burn calories throughout the day.

Tip: If you wish to make the most of your morning workout routine, focus on cardio activities.

The Moods Improve

Exercising release the feel-good hormones called endorphins in our bodies. These tend to proliferate after an exercise routine of sufficient duration and intensity. One does not have to do rigorous cardio to feel good; any workout done consistently would accomplish that.

Once you develop a routine, there wouldn't be a better way to start off your day. It boosts your mood and rewards you with a sense of accomplishment that can automatically make your day better.

Fitness may seem about feeling healthy and looking good, and it is, but ultimately it is about empowerment. If you commit to a fitness lifestyle and change all your bad habits to good ones, and make time to workout, eat right, and learn to find the fun in it all, you will amaze yourself with what you can accomplish. Those accomplishments will give you a sense of empowerment.

Accomplishments will come in many forms. You will lose weight; you will put on muscle. If you dedicate yourself to a little bit of bodybuilding, you may go so far as to sculpt your body into a stunning form. You can develop a fitness workout routine that will build your body just as you imagined it might be if you could use it to happen. Making your dreams become a reality if only in your appearance, can be a wonderful feeling that you get to feel every morning when you look in the mirror.

You will get stronger, possibly stronger than you ever thought possible. It will translate into your real life as things that were once daunting or difficult will seem effortless. You can be a lean, mean, powerful machine. You will even be surprised how strong you can be without being bulky or muscle-bound.

You may even go so far as to challenge yourself with new sports. Maybe you'll run in a 5km race or maybe a marathon. Will you do a mini-triathlon? Join a soccer team? Learn to play hockey? Maybe you'll take up dancing? The possibilities will seem endless. It will make you feel like a kid again as you make "playing" part of your life. You can customize your fitness workout routine to help you accomplish just about any physical goal.

Tired of feeling like a helpless passenger in your life? Life can be crazy, but fitness is one of those things that we can all control. At first, fitness will just be something you do to look and feel better. When that initial urge starts to wear thin, and you consider falling back into the same or bad habits, think about what you are giving up.

Billionaires have a Winning Routines

What is the fuss about winning the game of life? Why is it so important? How can feeling like a winner affect you?

I would like to share with you a very simple method that I have come to call 'consideration-check time.' It has quickly grown to be a vital part of my ever-expanding life.

Perhaps you can make it part of yours.

It is so powerful and effective that I find myself looking forward to the end of the evening. I still, to this day, perform this routine without fail and have been doing so for quite some years now. I am sure you, too, will enjoy it and reap its increasing rewards.

So what is it that I do, that is having me winning the game of life? What ceremonial procedure do I routinely practice every single evening that has tremendous results on how I think, feel and act?

The fantastic, easy-to-do, enriching routine that I habitually perform every evening is outlined below:

Thirty minutes before I go to bed, I take out my pen and notebook, then I sit back and close my eyes. I spend the next few minutes considering all my actions of the day.

I purposefully think back from the moment I opened my eyes to the present moment. I quietly contemplate my entire day, in full detail, where I recapture all my achievements, no matter how small and no matter in what area.

I keep those successes bubbling in my mind, bringing them more to life, reliving the experience. I stimulate those great winning feelings.

At the peak of my invigorated winning feelings, I open my eyes and write down how fantastic I feel, how strong and powerful I am, how I believe I can achieve all that I want and desire. When I finish,

I anchor the moment by clenching my right fist and declaring: "Yes. That's me!"

This awareness of exaggerated stimulus propels and spurs me to accomplish more. It feeds and prompts me with encouragement, motivation, and determination.

This way, I retire to bed feeling significantly powerful, wiser and more aware, in touch with my inner strengths and talents.

The next day, I feel revamped and energized. Strong and capable. Ready to accomplish more, feeling like an unstoppable winner. A winner all set and geared for more success.

That's how you become part of the team that is constantly winning the game of life. Are you willing to develop and maintain a winning feeling by writing down your daily successes, small or large, and replaying them in your mind?

CHAPTER 4

LIFE SKILLS BILLIONAIRES MASTER

Making Decisions

Influencing decision makers is a strategy that needs to be studied and scrutinized to be effective. The strategy requires the need to understand the different loops and holes in a company's decision-making process, including the decision-makers. You have to know and understand the different factors of how the decisions are made to be able to understand the whole process. It is also important that understanding these factors that influence the process is important to understanding what decisions are made the factors that influence the process may also affect the outcomes. Here are the four major factors of major decision making.

When you are faced with a decision-making situation, how do you go about it? Do you decide right there and then or do you postpone your decision up to some point?

While many experts recommend that a decision made quickly has many advantages, it can also lead to blunders. And many decisions are irreversible, if not leading to unpleasant outcomes. A systematic way should be applied to get the most of your decision.

Certainly, good decisions arise from a good understanding of the decision situation. If you do not fully understand or there is a lot of uncertainty in your mind, numbers can help you improve the outcome of your decision.

How does this technique work? The method is simple. Follow the steps below.

How to Improve Decision Making Skills

Step 1. List the advantages and disadvantages of your decision

Get a sheet of paper, make a two-column layout and write 'Advantages' at the left column and the right column, the 'Disadvantages.' List down all the advantages and disadvantages you can think of related to your decision.

Step 2. Rate your list of advantages and disadvantages

Rate each advantage or disadvantage you have listed using a 10-point scale ranging from unimportant to very important. If the advantage or disadvantage is unimportant, you may just rate it '1' but if you believe it is a major advantage or disadvantage, you may rate it a maximum of '10' points. If it is neither unimportant nor very important, your rate will be between the extremes.

Step 3. Add all the points

Sum up the points you gave for each advantage or disadvantage of your decision. From the total number of points, you will easily see which column has more points than the other. You may adopt the one with the greater number of points.

If the points are more or less similar, you may retry the steps again without referring to the earlier one. This is called iteration. You may do this three times to confirm your decision.

Evaluating Your Decision

After applying the steps above and arriving at a decision where the advantages are greater than the disadvantages, evaluate your decision by answering the following questions.

1. Is your decision urgently needed?

Do you need to make that decision? If not, then it is better to give more time to ponder your decision. Uncertainty is reduced with the passing of time. Procrastination can offer more opportunities to clear up issues.

2. Is your decision life changing?

What decisions is life changing? Deciding to marry or changing your job are examples. This involves life-long commitment or giving up an equally important choice so you must seriously think about the consequences of your decision.

3. Who will be affected by your decision?

If the only person who will be affected by the decision is you, then your decision should be quick. If something goes wrong, there is no one to blame but you. If your decision affects others, it will be wise to consult them, too.

Steps to making the right decision at the right time

Know Your Opponent:

If your Procrastination Time has a motto, it is, "Ignore it and it will go away!" This voice can be very quiet, but very persuasive. By keeping hyper-alert, you can catch this message before it sinks in. Then, when that thought crosses your mind, you can instantly label it as a distortion, and align yourself with reality. Rationally, you do know that the more you put unwanted tasks out of your mind, the more unfinished business accumulates! Soon, you simply cannot tie up all the loose ends as well as you would like. Let yourself take in how unpleasant this really feels.

Why Procrastinate?

You build strength by understanding your personal motivation to procrastinate. Then you can create the perfect antidote. So, which payoff tempts you the most? Here are just a few examples:

* Perhaps procrastinating steals enough time from your projects to let you dive into something you truly enjoy. Moreover, you put the price you must pay out of your mind.

* Maybe forgetting your challenge feels better than facing it squarely... at least, temporarily.

* You might rationalize that you work "best" under pressure. Although deep inside, you know that the final product suffers.

Make a list of what excuses you give yourself when you set important tasks aside.

Remember that no matter how you numb out what the future will bring, the unfinished business still poisons your pleasure!

Breaking the Procrastination Time Deadlock:

Since the Procrastination Time gets strength from creeping under your rational radar, your best defense is to shine a spotlight on its messages and to expose the myths.

To create an antidote to the Procrastination Time , ask yourself:

1. If you continue to procrastinate, what losses will you face?
2. If you continue to procrastinate, what additional work will you need to do to make up for lost time?
3. If you decide to stop procrastinating, what will end? Will you stop nagging yourself?
4. If you decide to stop procrastinating, what will begin? What first step can you commit to right now? Any movement towards your true goal, however small that step may be, points you in the right direction! You have your best energies working for you.

Throughout your question and answer sessions, maintain a friendly and supportive attitude towards yourself. Make it easy to confide in yourself when you are struggling with temptations! Then, you will get an instant alert when your Procrastination Time says, "Just forget about it."

You do yourself such a big favor when you handle your Procrastination Time with firmness! Nothing is better for your confidence than knowing you are willing to take good care of yourself in the world as it is.

Billionaires Prioritize their Activities

You know the rest. When we feel like we're perpetually behind and can't catch up, it's easy to blame our circumstances, jobs, and just about anything as long as it's not ourselves. After all, change is hard and, when we acknowledge our shortcomings as the reason for our inefficacy, the only logical next step is to do something about it (change). But rather than getting stuck on the hamster wheel of guilt, self-imposed pressure and feeling like a failure, most of us choose the path of least resistance - we stay behind, keep struggling, and continue blaming external factors. Why? Because, as I said, change is hard.

There Are Ways to Reclaim Your Productivity

And they don't have to be difficult. The beautiful thing about self-propelled change is that you can control it, direct it, and bite off as much or as little as you think can handle at once. Baby steps, anyone? As Stephen Covey tells us, "The key is not to prioritize what's on your schedule but to schedule your priorities." You don't need to hire a time management coach or personal assistant, and you can spare yourself the meltdown. With a little bit of basic, self-taught goal setting, time management techniques and regular mental pep talks (or out loud in the mirror, if that's what you're into) to keep yourself motivated and accountable, you'll be adequately equipped to catch up and get ahead.

Action Steps

Many of us are masters of the first two steps, awareness and pondering. We know we're behind, we wonder why, and we even tell ourselves we're going to fix it somehow. But then the cycle repeats itself, something unexpected happens, and we stumble over those first two steps again and again instead of progressing to the third. Want to know why? It's because there's a gap between the second and third steps. The space between your current situation and your metamorphosis into an effective individual is called the intention-behavior gap, and it can be bridged. The keys to crossing over to the other side are reprioritization and ownership, which are the areas where we most often fail (and the place where excuses go to die). We're all granted the same 24 hours in a day and, as unjust as that may seem, you can't appeal to the powers that be for more. Sure, some of us are busier than others. But there are solutions to any problem and, more often than not, the solutions begin with us.

Reprioritization and the Intention-Behavior Gap

We all have good intentions. But those intentions mean nothing when we fail to speak the "how" steps into existence, and we're not the only ones affected. There are consequences when you manage yourself and your schedule poorly. You aren't doing yourself or your health any favors, and you certainly aren't doing your loved ones any favors either. Don't you want to chip in and do your part of becoming healthier, calmer, and therefore positively impact the lives of your loved ones because they're getting more of you, too?

Redirect

Whether or not you have the luxury of being able to delegate, most of us don't like to. Anyone else subscribes to the belief that if you want something done right, you should do it yourself? (I can imagine a room full of raised hands.) But even without delegates or subordinates, anyone can redirect. Don't think of it as putting something off, ignoring something, or cutting corners. Think of it as reserving more resources for that item and giving it your full attention at an ideal time. Think of it as doing yourself and the item in question a favor by clearing your mind and plate of other things so that you can better focus on that one.

And don't forget one of the most crucial components of redirection - taking the necessary time to fuel yourself so that you can function optimally when addressing your agenda. Too many of us are guilty of "forgetting" to stop and eat lunch ("the day got away from me"), or forgoing lunch altogether to work throughout the afternoon because we feel like we can't afford to take a short break. This is extremely detrimental to your health, mood, well-being, and capacity to perform at high levels. Sacrificing yourself for the sake of your work will cause you more stress, put you even more behind, and catch up to you, even if it doesn't look like it at the moment. Next time you're tempted to give up your lunch break, weigh the long-term effects of that continued behavior against the short-term gain you might feel from completing a task. Then imagine yourself completing that task more efficiently after taking a small break to replenish your energy. You are not a robot - don't try to function as a machine by denying yourself basic human needs.

You should have the patience and the ability to know the capabilities in yourself. Then only you can manage it well. Keep your important things in the first place, even all those activities from which you are afraid or feeling lazy, finish that work first. Always enjoy your work which makes you feel comfortable and completing it successfully within time. If you get exhausted from your work, then you should spend some time with your family, as they should be given equal priority. You can participate in your children activities, can complete their homework with them and can visit your friends and relatives place.

Prioritizing your life can also be set by estimating all your work and the time to complete it. Make the list of all work and try to complete it successfully. You will have to first change your attitude towards work. If you see your work as a burden, then you cannot concentrate on it, but if you will start with the intention that you will enjoy it, then you can complete it on time as well as successfully.

Are you overworked, over scheduled? If you feel that your life is in a state of disorder, then you do not have to worry at all. Everything can be improved. Just prioritize your life by giving your time to those that are important to you, but again with some limits. Sometimes it happens that people got so much exhausted that they need a change. For that, they should do whatever they like to do. You just know your goals and intentions that what you want to do in your life, whether you have to give your 26 hours a day to it. And that is not impossible at all. The truth is after achieving your goal; you will also feel confident that you can achieve everything in your life. You have to do your work with full honesty.

That is why it is said that we should make a timetable for work that we must complete. Prioritize them according to your need. You will surely get all the way to do it. So time always runs according to us. We do not run according to the time, but we spend the time according to our ease.

Start your Day with Positivity

Definition of POSITIVITY.

1. The quality or state of being positive.
1. Something that is positive.

Sometimes in life, we go through stages where everything seems to be blank, and there is no way out. This is the time when you need positivity the most. The goal is to build the wall of positivity so high around you that no matter what negativity comes your way it cannot get through but bounces off and no longer affects your wellbeing. So today, we all shall take a pledge. Pledge, of being positive not only for ourselves but also for others.

How to be positive:

1. Surround yourself with positive people.
2. Try to see the positive aspect of all the situations.

* SURROUND YOURSELF WITH POSITIVE PEOPLE

We all know a person is affected the most by the company he keeps. Surround yourself with individuals who are going to lift you higher. This can change your outlook on life. If you like someone expresses it let them know about it. However, if you see it is not the same from that side. Back off. Because that person cannot see the best of you and will bring out the negativity in you. The one meant for you will come all the way only for you to your way. Once you let go of negative people, positive ones appear. Keep away from those who try to belittle your ambitions.

Only a few people in life will make you feel that you too can become great. Care for those who care for you. Stay with people who think you are important in their life. In a day, surround yourself with people who love you, motivate you, encourage you and just make you feel good about being you. Surround yourself with people who know your worth. You do not need too many people to be happy, just a few real ones who appreciate you for exactly who you are. Positivity brings happiness. Be happy that when others look at you, they become happy too. Smile and make others smile. Inspire others.

Be the inspiration for others. Be the type of person that other look at you and say I did not give up because of you. Life is too short to wake up with regrets. Love the people who treat you right and forget the ones who do not! If you get a chance take it.If it changes your life, let it. Nobody said life would be easy. They just said it would be worth it. Trust yourself, you have survived a lot. You will survive what is coming)

EVERYTHING HAPPENS FOR A REASON.

Try to see the positive aspects of all the situations. Life is not the way it is supposed to be. It is the way it is the way we cope with it that makes the difference. Stay positive even when it feels like your life is falling apart. Stop over-thinking everything. It is all going to be perfect at the end. We all are familiar with the happy ending concept.

Personally, believe that everything happens for a reason. People change so that you can learn to let go, things go wrong so that you can appreciate when they are right, you believe lies so that you eventually learn to trust no one but yourself, and sometimes-good things fall apart so better things can fall together. Make mistakes.

There is nothing wrong in making mistakes. Learn from it. Let others learn from your mistakes too. Do not always take negativity out of people. Understand them. Think positive. When God pushes you to the edge of difficulty, have faith, because only two things can happen either he will catch you when you fall, or he will teach you how to fly. Thinking positive does not mean expecting the best to happen every time, it is about accepting that whatever happens is best for this moment.

Sometimes the best thing you can do is not think, not wonder, not imagine, and not obsess. Just breathe and have faith that everything will work out for the best. Someday everything will make sense, so, for now, laugh at the confusion, smile through the tears and keep reminding yourself that everything happens for a reason.

Would you say that you just are personally motivated or are you currently waiting for one thing to come along and motivate you to action? Are you able to dig deep inside and uncover that spark or do you have to be prodded from the outside?

Have you ever sat down and introspect about it? Do you stagnate from a lack of motivation? Do you feel like you might be stuck in a rut and you are just going via the motions...one particular foot in front with the other?

What gets you out of bed in the morning? Is it the thought of accomplishing something wonderful and amazing or is it a swift kick to the rear?

What keeps you going when issues aren't going appropriately? Do own a goal in mind that you just can see with clarity and are actively taking every day methods to reach?

Can a Lack of Motivation be Overcome

It is important to discover one thing which you want irrespective of the difficulties you encounter when trying to accomplish it. That way you are going to continue to strive through the troubles. Inside the process, do factors that you appreciate to help break the routine of the work so, which you remain refreshed and focused and steer clear of burning out.

If you wish to steer clear of and defeat a lack of motivation, find out how to take pleasure in the method and not only the destination. What do you enjoy performing that keeps you moving towards the light in the end at the tunnel?

Concentration Assists in Forcing a Lack of Motivation Away

These are the items you have to preserve in front of you.

Contemplate on what you would like to attain...NOT on what you have not!

Make sure that you simply can't forget why you do what you do. Hang photos where you can see them each day, envisioning the completed result you've got in thought.

Visualize your dreams.

Make your dreams tangible. See them so typically that you can't aid but believe that they've currently happened. See them so obviously that when you reach your targets, it isn't even a surprise due to the fact you've already noticed it occur. Simultaneously, keep yourself-connected to what's occurring now. Bear in mind who you need to arrive at your destination with. Envision the future but do not get so caught up in it which you forget your present.

Ensure you invest time together with the people you love or when you reach your objective and obtain your dream they might not want to invest time with you. Do issues often that enable you to relax and clear your thinking; get outside, physical exercise read a great book or pay a visit to someplace new. For all those of us determined to achieve, sometimes it's easy to forget that we require to step back and get pleasure from life right now, too. It's not about becoming lazy or forgetting our responsibilities but concerning the want to recharge our batteries and be sure we don't just burn out. At times, we need just to step back and take a deep breath and unwind.

The choice is up to you.

Just bear in mind, it's crucial to be correct to who you are. Don't forget the people who have helped you get to exactly where you might be. Take pleasure in life along the way! That way once you get to the finish of the journey you won't wonder what happened to the life you did not reside. Look for methods to improve your productivity but allow you the freedom of rest.

In case you are searching for methods to achieve your monetary objectives and nevertheless be capable of residing your life, take a look at this critique of the Empower Network. http://tinyurl.com/73d4pvbIt is goal will be to help you make a living although still living life. Don't remain a victim of a lack of motivation...Find Your Objective!

They Create A Plan of Action

Each day hundreds of people type into their favorite search engines the question, "What is Personal Development?" hoping to find the key to self-improvement and personal growth. Unfortunately, they find very few answers to that question, but we are going to change that right here by detailing the key components to improving your life.

OK, in simple terms, Personal Development is the actions you take to improve some or all the aspects of your life, including your health, finances, attitude, fitness and education. Self-improvement is one part of personal growth that deals with becoming the person you aspire to be whether physically, mentally or spiritually.

I know that this is not getting to the heart of your question, but bear with me for a minute.

There are a multitude of resources to help you in your quest for personal development, including books, CDs, DVD, seminars, life coaches and professional mentors, but do not overlook family and friends who have your best interest at heart.

Personal Development begins with dissatisfaction with where you are currently in some aspect of your life. As your dissatisfaction increases, a burning desire to change that part of your life leads to action that will eventually produce the desired improvement. Self-improvement is a process that takes time. It is not just a single action or series of actions, like reading a self-help book or attending motivational seminars. It is an attitude change that requires discipline and commitment.

Wow, so that is the cut and dry answer to what is Personal Development? But you do not care about that factual answer so much, do you? You want to focus in on your own self-improvement.

Let us talk about what is personal growth for you!

Let us begin to look at how you can achieve the improvement you want in your life. The first step to lasting personal change and development is putting together your plan of action called a Development Plan (PDP). This will become your road map to success. It will establish your clearly defined goals and the steps you need to take to accomplish them.

A Development Plan is always a work in progress. As you complete one task, you will need to add new growth and educational opportunities to your plan. Before we begin to put this plan together, you need to answer a very important question that only you can answer. The question is "WHY?"

Why are you seeking personal growth?
Why do you want to change?
Why do you feel you need to change?
Why are you not content with who and what you are now?
What is Personal Development for you?

Well, the answers to these "WHY?" questions will help you to determine the level of Desire you have for making these changes.

Without desire and a burning passion to change you will not get far in creating your Development Plan. Moreover, without your PDP, your "road map", you will not succeed in making changes because you will not stay on track long enough to accomplish anything meaningful.

Okay, I am assuming you have adequately answered the entire "WHY?" questions and you have confirmed your desire to make the necessary changes in your life. Now we are ready to begin to put together the Development Plan that will dramatically change your life. I can hear you saying it now, "Whoa, dramatically change my life? I am just looking for a little improvement and not a massive change".

Hey, here is the deal: if you are going to take the time to think about and write your PDP, then you better be thinking about a dramatic change that will get you motivated and excited or otherwise you will lose focus quickly. Trust me; I have been there like so many others. People who need to lose five or 10 pounds do not get too motivated, but the person who needs to lose 40, 50 or more pounds gets motivated by a burning desire that cannot easily be quench. Baby, they are on Fire to achieve their Desire!

These people understand what self-improvement is all about. They understand it takes a passionate commitment and burning desire to get the results they want with their body and their health.

So back to the point, if you are going to write a detailed Development Plan then you need to be thinking in terms of major life-changing goals. So we know you have the desire and motivation to seek self-improvement change in your life. Let us begin to put together a plan itself.

Start by getting a thin spiral notebook that you will only use for this purpose. This notebook will become your own personal playbook or, maybe better yet, your own personal Business Plan that you will use to build the new and improved you with over the next few weeks, months and years.

Now that you have that spiral notebook open it up to the first page and write the words, My Primary Goals and Mission in Life, across the top of the page. This goal and mission statement states where you want to be in your life, NOT where you currently are now.

This is what you will return to on a daily basis to remind you of where you are going. This mission statement must be as detailed and specific as you can make it. Be creative and do not limit yourself in your thinking, but make sure you are realistic.

The next part of your Development Plan is the self-assessment part where you have to determine exactly where you are now and what you want to improve.

Finally, you need to make a list of all the areas in your life you want to make a significant improvement. Be very specific in establishing your goals. As an example, it is not enough to say you want to lose some weight. You have to say I want to lose 30 pounds by December 31 of this year through a low-fat diet and aerobic exercise program at the YMCA. This detailed goal written out in your PDP will help you stay focused and on track.

Now it is time for you to get started by writing down your first personal growth goals, then start taking the action necessary to make them a reality.

Always Think Big

Big thinking combined with coming up short and quitting is a disaster. Big thinking combined with genuine persistence, even when the going gets strange or rough is a success. Here is how. Think about this: Most people, and I do mean most people, when things get strange, tough or both strange and tough, quit or fear thoughts get the best of them. But most of the best people, and that is very few people: they fail seemingly endlessly and then get over with genuine success once or a few times and then become legends. It is like George Herman "Babe" Ruth and his home run record versus his baseball hitting attempt records. He had more attempts at home run hitting than he made actual successful home run hitting. But, what do we remember a record of? We remember a record of all the successful home run hitting.

This is a better example: Thomas Edison and his assistants reportedly failed over ten thousand times with many of the inventions before they worked fully successfully once and always through a fixed formula that would work repeatedly, but the full success of that one fixed formula versus the many failures before it, made Thomas Edison and those associated with him, legends. My point? A legend becomes a legend through big goals, and gigantic seeming failures, and then ultimate success through persistence. After all, what was the real point of "The Odyssey of

Homer" and "Beowulf" as the ancient epic poems that they were? These stories showed this reality of massive failure, then even greater successfully. Although, they had many seeming myths, and seeming silly and antiquated concepts that can be misunderstood, the successful fully understand what those myths represented in reality. Life is an obstacle course with all those monsters, wars and active obstacles at a deeply subliminal level or a not at all overt level.

So, here is the importance of thinking big when you can fully back it up with action and persistence in that order. To succeed big, you have to fail big a few times to fully understand how and why to succeed after those failures or "experiments" and tries. First, you learn and then you succeed, to put it another way. Winning is easy when given to a person or inherited without effort, but when you want to become a genuine big thinker and genuine legend through your efforts, it is very hard, because of the factors I am writing about.

To end, Napoleon Hill once had an essay on seeming failure and ultimate success. He put forth the same realities I am putting out, only in somewhat different words. So, I will end by paraphrasing his sentence: "Woe to the person that cannot find lessons in seeming failure for that ultimate genuine success."

There are certain things about thinking big, winning and losing I wish I could fill in. But, I cannot. For you need to perceive and think for yourself to find those things inside and outside this article. Inside this article "between the lines." You fully find those things outside this article through experience and understanding fully on your own.

The generation of an idea depends upon the way you think. The person who thinks big tends to generate big and innovative ideas comparing to other people. The person must have courage and ability to hold on to the big idea to be able to achieve big things. For example, the people with a big vision always try to think of the big idea which will earn them respect and fame and this is the reason they bring out innovative ideas which will help them to achieve big things in life. There are failures in the people's life who think big, but the major point is to hold on to a vision. Failures help you to learn lots of things to bring out better ways to achieve your goals.

The first step you should do to have the courage to think big is to find what you love. The people who don't have interest in a particular subject cannot create the creative ideas which will help them to achieve their goal. The way to find out what you love is to analyze your skills and knowledge. You will have to explore what you love. You should first analyze your performance in different subjects before you can find what you love. You can even ask your friends to know what you're good at to explore your subject of interest. This will help you to develop the feeling of passion and curiosity which will play a vital part to develop the courage to think big and set a big vision. After you find your subject of interest, study about the life of the great people who have achieved big things in the particular subject which will provide you the confidence to achieve big things on that subject.

When you suffer from the failure in trying something new, just remember the life of great people who have failed many times before they have achieved big things in their life, this will encourage you to hold on and learn from your failure. For example, a great person like Albert Einstein faced lots of criticism in his idea for other people. When you think big, you will have a vision which will help you to achieve big things in life. Your curiosity and passion will help you to achieve big things in your life which is the reason you must have the courage to hold on and learn. Curiosity will help you to explore new and innovative ideas which will help you to achieve bigger things in life. Always remember that every great thing was new at some point in time and those achievements are the result of having a big vision.

They have Visions and Ideals

There can be no ambiguity about the vision. Too many leaders have fuzzy vision, but obscurity in the vision will not encourage and mobilize others. A vision is not something abstract: it is a clear picture of what the organization can realistically accomplish. When explaining the vision, leaders must word the vision in simple terms. It is not a theological treatise or an academic paper. What are we looking to achieve? By the time we're finished explaining, everyone should be able to see where we are going. To that end, leaders must solicit questions. In casting the vision, we will not communicate all the details (that's a matter of strategic planning), but by responding to questions, we ensure that people truly understand what we are aiming for.

The purpose is the why; vision is the what; the goal is the how. As we continue to communicate the vision, we will address these three areas. The purpose is important: we have to know why we're doing what we're doing, or else vision is an exercise in futility. Goals are the intentional steps that we have to take to realize the vision. Without such steps, vision is simply a dream, an ethereal idea that dissipates when we wake up to reality.

To communicate the vision, we have to thoroughly think it out. Good ideas don't become vision until we submit to this process. There are many things that we have to think about. We need to determine what resources are needed and whether we can access those resources. We have to think about the result or results. We have to think about sustainability and continuity unless the vision is simply for a one time event. We have to think about the potential benefits and weigh them against the disadvantages. We must also consider the time frame. When we communicate the vision to others, they may be involved in the thinking process, but they also want to know that we have thought things through. It is first our vision before it becomes theirs.

If the vision is somewhat new to the organization, our core leaders can assess the clarity of the vision. It is a mistake to share the vision with our subordinates before sharing it with our fellow leaders. Some leaders in their zeal bypass their leadership team and tell the world what they intend to do. This can foster serious fallout and is premature. Our core leaders can help us in drafting the vision, reworking and refining it until it is fully mature and ready to be presented to the rest of the organization.

Leaders must be creative in communicating the vision. Presenting the vision, in the same way, can bore people. Contemporary society, for good or for bad, is accustomed to many types of media: different styles appeal to different people. Additionally, the leader doesn't have to be the only one who communicates the vision - main influencers can also share the vision. This allows influencers to take ownership of the vision, and it also allows the leaders to work with others since no one leader can connect with everyone. Creativity involves knowing the people in your organization and what appeals to them.

The vision must be communicated continually. Some leaders make the mistake of thinking that people have grasped the vision when it has been presented once or a few times. Vision statements can be included in all the publications and correspondence of the organization: letters, emails, banners, posters are some of the tools that can be used. Leaders should speak on the vision at least once a month. This allows people to take ownership of the vision, to know and understand what the vision involves. Meetings and promotions can be used to communicate the vision. Once the vision is being continually communicated, people can connect their actions to the vision. They can assess whether what they are doing facilitates the realization of the vision.

Leaders must connect the past to the present and the future. Connecting with the past brings about a sense of continuity: it helps people that were with the organization for a while feeling a part of. Newer people need to understand and appreciate the organization's history. Present actions determine the momentum of the vision. The present is critical: the past is unchangeable but the present is not. We have to be intentional in what we do - present actions lay the foundation for the future: an ability to focus on the present separates the movers from the dreamers. Without a vision for the future, we can end up being activity driven, just doing things with no real objective in mind. The future has to do with what we hope to accomplish.

Leaders must be able to connect with the people in both communicating and realizing the vision. There must be a relationship: first with the primary influencers and leaders then with others in the organization. This happens by spending time with them and listening to them. Connecting with people involves having a warm and friendly disposition. When leaders speak, they can connect through using illustrations, stories, anecdotes, analogies that are familiar and loved by the people and appropriate humor. They can connect by speaking in a reasonable amount of time (too short or too long is ineffective), dealing with what's on people's heart, speaking in inclusive terms "we," and calling people to and believing in their greatness. Leaders have to communicate concern for people more than for an agenda.

Leaders are often confronted with the dilemma of wanting to and knowing the importance of their vision, and how to realistically explain it so that others will share that vision. There is often a fine line between being a visionary and motivating others to vital action, on the one hand, and being realistic and practical, maintaining priorities within the constraints of the present circumstances and realities of an organization.

1. Why is it so important and essential for a leader to have a vision? To a great degree, because it is that vision that makes the individual a leader, because it permits him to envision what others do not yet grasp, and set priorities and plans of action that plan not only to address present needs but also longer term ones. Great leaders see things as they should be but must transform those visions into definitive action. It is the sign of a real leader that he can remain grounded and approachable, and seem safe to his constituents (in other words, not scare them off or have them consider him too extreme) while creating parameters and propelling his group towards his vision. Anyone can be elected to a position of leadership, but few become great and important leaders. A visionary leader can turn around a flailing organization and help it regain its focus and direction, by leading them to an evolutionary progression.

2. When a leader can transform a group in an evolutionary manner, he maximizes his chances of others accepting his ideas. He must calmly, logically, and in a motivating manner explain to others why his vision is more than simply and ideal or some alternative, but rather something that is vital to the group if it is to maintain its relevance. In other words, he must demonstrate and communicate calmly and logically why this vision enhances the group and maximizes its chances of sustainability. This takes skill and preparation, because people are far more liable to follow and agree with the idea that they consider logical, gradual

and evolutionary, than they would to follow something they believe to be revolutionary.

Vision has to do with leaders and organizations' ability to see what they want to accomplish. It is like building a house: the house plan and a drawing of the house show what the finished product will look like. When the house is completed, it is expected that it will look essentially like the plan and the drawing. There may be cosmetic changes, but there will be no major differences.

There can be no ambiguity about the vision. Too many leaders have fuzzy vision, but obscurity in the vision will not encourage and mobilize others. A vision is not something abstract: it is a clear picture of what the organization can realistically accomplish. When explaining the vision, leaders must word the vision in simple terms. It is not a theological treatise or an academic paper. What are we looking to achieve? By the time we're finished explaining, everyone should be able to see where we are going. To that end, leaders must solicit questions. In casting the vision, we will not communicate all the details (that's a matter of strategic planning), but by responding to questions, we ensure that people truly understand what we are aiming for.

The purpose is the why; vision is the what; the goal is the how. As we continue to communicate the vision, we will address these three areas. The purpose is important: we have to know why we're doing what we're doing, or else vision is an exercise in futility. Goals are the intentional steps that we have to take to realize the vision. Without such steps, vision is simply a dream, an ethereal idea that dissipates when we wake up to reality.

To communicate the vision, we have to thoroughly think it out. Good ideas don't become vision until we submit to this process. There are many things that we have to think about. We need to determine what resources are needed and whether we can access those resources. We have to think about the result or results. We have to think about sustainability and continuity unless the vision is simply for a one time event. We have to think about the potential benefits and weigh them against the disadvantages. We must also consider the time frame. When we communicate the vision to others, they may be involved in the thinking process, but they also want to know that we have thought things through. It is first our vision before it becomes theirs.

If the vision is somewhat new to the organization, our core leaders can assess the clarity of the vision. It is a mistake to share the vision with our subordinates before sharing it with our fellow leaders. Some leaders in their zeal bypass their leadership team and tell the world what they intend to do. This can foster serious fallout and is premature. Our core leaders can help us in drafting the vision, reworking and refining it until it is fully mature and ready to be presented to the rest of the organization.

Leaders must be creative in communicating the vision. Presenting the vision, in the same way, can bore people. Contemporary society, for good or for bad, is accustomed to many types of media: different styles appeal to different people. Additionally, the leader doesn't have to be the only one who communicates the vision - main influencers can also share the vision. This allows influencers to take ownership of the vision, and it also allows the leaders to work with others since no one leader can connect with everyone. Creativity involves knowing the people in your organization and what appeals to them.

The vision must be communicated continually. Some leaders make the mistake of thinking that people have grasped the vision when it has been presented once or a few times. Vision statements can be included in all the publications and correspondence of the organization: letters, emails, banners, posters are some of the tools that can be used. Leaders should speak on the vision at least once a month. This allows people to take ownership of the vision, to know and understand what the vision involves. Meetings and promotions can be used to communicate the vision. Once the vision is being continually communicated, people can connect their actions to the vision. They can assess whether what they are doing facilitates the realization of the vision.

Leaders must connect the past to the present and the future. Connecting with the past brings about a sense of continuity: it helps people that were with the organization for a while feeling a part of. Newer people need to understand and appreciate the organization's history. Present actions determine the momentum of the vision. The present is critical: the past is unchangeable but the present is not. We have to be intentional in what we do - present actions lay the foundation for the future: an ability to focus on the present separates the movers from the dreamers. Without a vision for the future, we can end up being activity driven, just doing things with no real objective in mind. The future has to do with what we hope to accomplish.

Leaders must be able to connect with the people in both communicating and realizing the vision. There must be a relationship: first with the primary influencers and leaders then with others in the organization. This happens by spending time with them and listening to them. Connecting with people involves having a warm and friendly disposition. When leaders speak, they can connect through using illustrations, stories, anecdotes, analogies that are familiar and loved by the people and appropriate humor. They can connect by speaking in a reasonable amount of time (too short or too long is ineffective), dealing with what's on people's heart, speaking in inclusive terms "we," and calling people to and believing in their greatness. Leaders have to communicate concern for people more than for an agenda.

One of the most frustrating things in life is to be part of an organization with no vision. You reflect on the years that you've been there and realize that the organization has made no real progress. This is a leadership problem. Leaders must take the time to develop a vision and must also evaluate to make sure that the vision is being realized. Time and resources are limited and must be strategically used to realize the vision.

They are Purpose Driven

We are in a new dispensation of time where people are evolving mentally, spiritually, etc. This is an era where the purpose is championed, in business, sports, movies, etc. Every organization has a plan and a purpose for its existence. It has its raison d'etre, without it there is no organization.

Organizations that are soaring have embedded their raison d'etre in all their activities. Sometimes it's blatantly clear and sometimes its a bit subtle. As the purpose gospel continues to take center stage, I have realized through my interactions with many people and also through traveling that while there is a greater number that talks about purpose, there is also a lesser number that walks out the purpose. It's not always easy to walk in one's purpose and many people continually discover that.

The key thing is to make a start. This means getting away from the hustle and bustle and all the 'noise' of life, and take a moment and ask who AM I, what was I born to do and where AM I going. Identity forms a key part in identifying the purpose. Many people have received their identity from other people as opposed to digging deep on the inside of themselves and 'figuring' themselves out. We are so much more than how people define us.

I have often found out that people define you by how they met you. If they met you as a clerk, in their minds you will always be a clerk. Although you could be so much more. So without knowing it's so easy to pick up how people define you and take that as your identity. This sometimes starts in our formative years, how our parents, sibling, friends, school teachers define us. However, it's up to us to decide how we ought to be defined and most importantly how we define ourselves. Sometimes it's not what people call you, but what you answer to.

Once you make that decision to align your life with the core and essence of who you are on the inside, life takes a different meaning. A purpose driven life is no longer just talk but a way of living. We see this in champions of all fields; Athletes don't do things for the sake of doing. They don't just eat anything; they choose their food with a purpose in mind. They purposely decide their diet, because they know the path of being a champion doesn't accommodate a careless diet. They exercise regularly to keep themselves fit, to the ordinary person this type of discipline can be daunting, but to the champion who has made his or her mind, this is no longer hard it becomes a way of life.

Movie actors who take up a script that requires a certain figure will take months of preparation to fit that body type. I was watching the interview that Emily Blunt did the other day, this was about her role in The Adjustment Bureau, she had scenes doing ballet dancing. In this interview, she mentioned that she had to spend several months doing ballet dancing classes and getting herself in the right figure. That is purpose right there, as an actress she had to selectively do certain things to play her role in the movie and manifest her purpose as an actress in the movie.

Wherever you may be on your journey towards destiny and purpose. Whether you have found it or still looking may I encourage you to take that moment and get on the inside and discover the real you. Not what people expect you to be, not what other people define you as not what you think other people want you to be. I am talking about the real you. Discovering the real you and allowing you to be you is often a key part in discovering the identity and ultimately a pivotal step towards finding purpose.

Do you think you are capable of living a life full of drive and purpose? Many people will shake their heads and say no, they're not. They will continue plodding along feeling dissatisfied with things, and they won't feel quite sure about how to resolve them.

It's okay if you aren't yet living a purpose driven life because you can change things whenever you want to so you can do this. It can help to look at how successful people live their lives. It doesn't matter what profession or walk of life they are in; they will always be living lives filled with purpose and meaning.

Aren't these people just lucky?

You may be tempted to think so, but this is not the case. It is simply that they are true to their purpose and they are living lives full of meaning. You can achieve amazing things in your ideal chosen field if you discover your purpose and go about making it a reality.

The difference between the successful people in each field and those who are unsuccessful is quite often perseverance. Even if you know what your purpose in life is, it may not always be a breeze to reach it and make it happen. No path is without its obstacles, and if you are ready to give up on the first one you encounter, you will not be living a life with purpose.

Successful people discover their purpose and work towards it diligently and with dedication. Every day when they wake up, the first thing on their mind is their purpose in life and how they are moving towards it. It lights them up, fires them up and leads them to do amazing things.

You are capable of just as much!

When you marry up with your ideal purpose in life, it changes you as a person. It makes you realize you are capable of making a difference in the world. Even if you are completely unsure what your purpose is at the moment, you can probably find clues to it in your life as it is now.

Take some time to think about your life and what you love to do. Ignore your job if you hate it; your purpose undoubtedly lies elsewhere. Think about every aspect of your life and see whether you can discover the clues that will lead you to your purpose. They will be there, and once you see them, you will be a step closer to living a purpose driven life.

It is never too late to change your life. Make today the first day in your quest to find and be faithful to your purpose. You will be glad you did.

Have Self-Control

It is important to know your limits of self-restraint, and a person's self-restraint is limited, and it can be consumed. Each morning you may be full of spirit and self-confidence, but in the afternoon, you tend to be unable to control the temper.

Do not crave for too much. Each time, you can change one bad habit. You will not be able to control the attacks the pressure in the life but what you can do is to select one bad habit at one time and overcome it. For example, when you are on a diet, do not try to quit drinking or to start a new job. If you venture for everything, you may achieve nothing.

Self-control is directly related to the glucose that has been consumed. If you feel your blood sugar level is low, you can find a low-calorie snack food, for example a small handful of blueberries or chopped nuts. Also, in this way, you can avoid some excuses you may think of for giving up your plan.

Don't be tied by normal regulations. You can choose to quit a bad habit when you are on holiday, for example smoking. Because when you are on vacation, you stay away from the people, events and places which will make you think of smoking the cigarettes. Each vacation may be a good chance for you to make some positive changes to your habits.

When you have set a goal, and after you have reached the target, you can reward yourself. Do not underestimate the role that incentives may play.

The reward indicates the approval, although it may be endowed by yourself. It does give you the psychological indication that your effort has not been spent in vain.

If you have made efforts to resist temptation, and then give up, your power of self-restraint will remain dry because you choose to give up after trying.

Self-discipline is a great self-improvement tool and a continuous procedure that delivers long lasting results. You can conquer any self-destructing routines and endow yourself for a far better life.

You will always find unforeseen circumstances, hindrances and problems on your journey towards attainment and success. To turn out successful, you must be strong and be determined. Along with the exceptional 100-day challenge review, let us take a look at the 5 most essential things that can help you master self-discipline.

The 5 basic strategies to learn self-discipline are:

1. Persistence: Never surrender, say no to your pessimism or negative thoughts, and ward off any self-defeating thoughts or lethargy. You should develop your tenacity and resistance power. Because of this, you can determine your route towards self-discipline. Once your plan is set in motion, absolutely nothing can keep you from climbing your ladder towards personal development.
2. Assume responsibility: Knowing your obligation is the initial step to increase your mental strength. Your sense of duty will push you to size up each of the areas where you should improve on and act accordingly.
3. Get Well organized: You need to act with assurance in every task that you consider. Have a prepared list of goals to perform along with a thorough course of action. Vow to yourself that you're going to finish a task in a particular time. This will not only provide you with the proper outlook, but this will also enable you to stop trying to escape from conflicts. Treat yourself for each moderate achievement. Pay attention to a single task at a time. Don't divert your attention and try to go as reported by your

definite plan. Start slowly, but steadily increase your pace while you gain your skills.

4. Visualize the outcome: Anytime you feel lethargic or bored, take a couple of deep breaths and ignore your tension and attempt to unwind for a short time. Pause and picture the actions in front of you as though they've been already completed. Assess the benefits or bonuses and feel the whole scene in every detail. It will encourage you to carry on with your next assignment. It will likewise prepare both of your unconscious and conscious minds for a more proactive and organized way of everyday living. Whenever you keep repeating the method, the encouragement to act will grow much stronger, until a firm behavior has formed.

5. Develop Willpower: Self-control is usually the pillar of strength. Although difficult to sustain, it will help you to handle your concerns strategically. Attempt to replicate your role models. This will be a source of inspiration so that you can advance in your endeavors for self-discipline.

Taking responsibility and carrying out tasks in an organized way may create remarkable outcomes. As stated by the successful 100-day challenge review, perfecting the art of self-discipline has become the key to achieving consistent self-improvement.

The process in which a person gains control over one's mind and subsequently influence their thinking, attitude, behavior, emotions or decision making is known as mind control. This term has various other aliases which are brainwashing, coercive persuasion, thought control, thought reform and systematic manipulation of psychological and social influence. When a person adapts this technique with full perfection, he can make anyone do things according to the manipulator's will. It is a form of hypnosis in cases where two parties are involved where in the victim of coercive persuasion can create new attitudes to do those things willingly which they formerly might have detested.

When the technique of mind control is practiced on oneself, it helps the individual in a variety of ways. It helps you to communicate with yourself and understand your capabilities that have been submerged within you all your life and finally to channel your strength and learn how to use it to your benefit. By aiding you in gaining total control of your emotions and thoughts thus developing self-control this technique is an ultimate life saver and proves to boost your inner confidence. You tend to use this balanced control on yourself to tackle any major difficulties you come across in life. This technique not just helps you gain self-control but also makes you so influential in the eyes of the people around you thus winning over their respect and eventually paving a way to a peaceful life.

It is rather easy to control other organs of your body like your eyes, hands, legs and so on wherein when you want to close your eyes your brain signals the eyes to be closed, and so it is done but when it comes to the mind, the moment you decide not to think of a certain thing, the mind thinks of it anyway. The moment you can manipulate your thinking according to your own will you can be successfully termed as a master of your consciousness. Hypnosis is one of the techniques of mind control where you experience a change in your thoughts and feelings and an alteration in your perception of certain things. In cases of extreme pain or hurt it can ask your mind to eliminate the pain which does prove to be so when you have total control of your mind. Thus mind control is effectively used as a painkiller and a way to alleviate anxiety. Sleeping and eating disorders can be cured using this technique. Techniques like self-hypnosis are one of the most effective mind control procedure practiced on one self that eventually helps you come out of a stressful situation, get rid of bad habits and addictions and inculcate self-motivation.

You also gain the ability to prevent some memories from occurring in your mind that might have caused an emotional disturbance in the past. Sometimes psychotherapists make their patients listen to recorded tapes of positive messages that are aimed at seeping in the positive thoughts into the patient's mind and thus changing their outlook towards certain things. Another mind control technique is to practice the silent treatment. At times there are people or situations that bother us to the extremes, but when you gain effective control of your mind, you tend to be neutral towards these unwanted elements in your life and try and be indifferent to what has been bothering you. By remaining indifferent, you attain peace of mind and instead make the others who create trouble for you wonder how well you handle the situation with your calm attitude. This behavior not only changes your way of thinking but also changes the way people approach you.

It is important to know your limits of self-restraint, and a person's self-restraint is limited, and it can be consumed. Each morning you may be full of spirit and self-confidence, but in the afternoon, you tend to be unable to control the temper.

Do not crave for too much. Each time, you can change one bad habit. You will not be able to control the attacks the pressure in the life but what you can do is to select one bad habit at one time and overcome it. For example, when you are on a diet, do not try to quit drinking or to start a new job. If you venture for everything, you may achieve nothing.

Self-control is directly related to the glucose that has been consumed. If you feel your blood sugar level is low, you can find a low-calorie snack food, for example, a small handful of blueberries or chopped nuts. Also, in this way, you can avoid some excuses you may think of for giving up your plan.

Don't be tied by normal regulations. You can choose to quit a bad habit when you are on holiday, for example, smoking. Because when you are on vacation, you stay away from the people, events, and places which will make you think of smoking the cigarettes. Each vacation may be a good chance for you to make some positive changes to your habits.

When you have set a goal, and after you have reached the target, you can reward yourself. Do not underestimate the role that incentives may play. The reward indicates the approval, although it may be endowed by yourself. It can give you the psychological indication that your effort has not been spent in vain.

If you have made efforts to resist temptation, and then give up, your power of self-restraint will remain dry because you choose to give up after trying.

They do not Procrastinate

Procrastination: the act of procrastinating; putting off or delaying or deferring an action to a later time.

This is simply one meaning of procrastination.

There are many other meanings and interpretations, but for the sake of simplicity, we will just use the above definition. How many of us "put off" until tomorrow what we should be doing today? It is believed that the majority of Americans procrastinate on a high scale every day.

Whenever we practice procrastination it destroys our productivity- killing our dreams. Just think for a minute: what can you possibly accomplish (that's worth accomplishing) if you fail to take action? If you put off cleaning your home, you will eventually be living in a pig pin, not to mention the health issues that can arise from poor maintenance.

Another version defines procrastination as "intentionally and habitually putting off what should be done." Notice that procrastination is intentional. So many people fool themselves into believing that procrastination is something that just "happens" without any human effort or contribution. This, however, is not true. You have to actively participate to procrastinate. When you know something needs to be done and you choose not to do it, you are actively participating in and causing your failure.

Imagine if you felt that your body was just not functioning properly and you made plans to go to the doctor. Your appointment arrives and because you felt like you worked hard all week and you deserved a little rest, you put it off. One day turns into one week, one week into a month, and finally, you just forget about going at all. After passing out at work, you find that you have a condition that could have been prevented if you would have just done what needed to be done.

Don't let procrastination kill your dreams of being a success.

There is no miracle solution for procrastination except to take action. Taking the necessary action when required to is the only solution for procrastination. Most people procrastinate when it's time to go to the gym or work out but report feeling better after going to the gym or exercising. Whenever you procrastinate, you are left feeling guilty and even depressed at times. People who lack the motivation to accomplish even minimal tasks have been found to be borderline depressed or manically depressed. You will always feel better after you get things done.

Procrastination adds to depression and can cause one to experience bad health, bad relationships, failing grades, and poor work performance which can lead to the loss of one's employment. No one wants to experience these things happening to them, so why do they procrastinate?

Recognizing Procrastination

The first step in overcoming procrastination is acknowledging that procrastination exist. You can't get to "victory" until you first recognize that you have a problem. It's kind of like having a medical issue. You cannot get the needed treatment that's required until you "first" acknowledge and diagnose the issue, then you can move on to treating the problem.

Establish "why" you procrastinate

Understanding the "why" behind your procrastination moves you closer to overcoming it. Let's say you are putting off cleaning your house. Maybe it's because you've allowed it to get so out of hand that it becomes overwhelming to you and you just wish it would go away. Usually, procrastination takes place whenever a task that needs to be done is not pleasurable. Most humans have no problem with getting things done that's pleasurable to them. It's human nature. We are designed to move away from pain and draw close to pleasure.

Four easy Steps to counter procrastination

Step #1

Mind shifting: since you recognize that humans are wired to move away from painful things, associate procrastination with the consequences of not getting important things done. Create a mental picture of the negative results that can occur if you don't get things done. This mental shift can give you the motivation to "take action" to avoid the pain of the consequences.

Step #2

Prioritize: Sometimes you may procrastinate because it seems like there's so much to do yet so little time to get things done. A way to overcome this type of procrastination is through prioritizing. Write down a "to-do" list and then look at it to see what tasks are most important and what tasks are least important. Then prioritize those tasks according to their importance level (1. being the most important while 10. being the least important)

Step #3

Accountability Partner: Appointing someone to hold you accountable is another great way to combat procrastination. We usually attempt to do what we say when we know that someone else is watching us and will hold us accountable.

Step #4

Plan ahead: This step can tie into step #2. Establish your priority "to do" list the night before. Accomplishing your list ahead of time can, first of all, give you a boost of confidence-since you've gotten something done. You may also find yourself sleeping better at night looking forward to the next day. Since we cannot predict with certainty the events of tomorrow, be prepared to change some things around on your list if need be.

You are on your way to VICTORY!!

Now that you are on your way to a happier, fuller life- don't resist the urge to celebrate your accomplishment. You deserve it!

CHAPTER 5

THE LIFESTYLES OF BILLIONAIRES: REAL VS. IMAGINED

The Difference Between Dreaming and Doing

One of the main reasons for the death of dreams is that people neglect to DO anything to start making their dreams into a reality. We allow fear, doubts, other people's opinions and procrastination stop us from doing what needs to be done.

Though it may seem like an uphill battle to make any go from dreaming to doing, there are some things you can do now to start you on the path toward the attainment of your heart's desire.

1) Do something every single day

There are often a ton of things necessary do to get you where you want to go. It can seem like so much that just thinking about it is enough to make you want to quit.

To remedy this, break the large task into smaller and more manageable tasks. Then, do something every single day to move you toward your ultimate goal.

For example, let's say you were trying to lose 20 pounds by a certain date. You know that wouldn't happen overnight. But if you eat right and go to the gym every day it seems like less daunting of a task.

The trick is to make sure that you do something every single day. If you do happen to miss a day, don't get discouraged. Just get right back on track the next day.

2) Have an accountability partner

Have you ever been extra motivated to accomplish some goal? For the first few days or weeks, everything goes great. You are doing something every day and seem to be making much progress. Then, all of a sudden, you lose motivation. You miss a day. Then another. Then another one. Pretty soon you have lost all progress and are back at square one.

Now imagine this undergoing the same process with someone who will check in on you every few days. They will make sure that you are on track and work toward your goal.

It's sometimes easy to let ourselves down, but when we get others involved, it ups the ante a bit. Let someone you trust in on your dream and your commitment to getting there. This is very powerful and can sometimes make all the difference in the world to between success and failure.

3) Set goals

If dreams are the ultimate destination, then goals are like roadmaps. Have you ever felt like you had a very busy day but then realized that you didn't get anything done? That is what trying to get to your destination without setting a goal is like. You want to make sure that you are making forward progress every day.

Set realistic goals. Fight the temptation to set a goal that is out of the realm of possibility for where you are currently. For example, if your goal is to learn to play the piano, you should have a goal to learn "Mary Had a Little Lamb" before you can play a classic by Mozart.

Fulfillment of the dream is your responsibility. Fulfillment is accomplished through the trifecta of desire, belief, and action. For these three elements to harmoniously balance together often requires inner work. Just to recognize this mystery is to begin to see life more clearly.

There is an unaware part of our being that governs (influences) our thinking, feelings, and actions. Although we may consciously want to manifest something wonderful in our life, we may at the same-time subconsciously sabotage our efforts.

Desire includes having, doing and being. Measure your desire to change your desire to remain the same. The mind will go along with the fantasy of dreaming while simultaneously resisting change. Old ruts may be uncomfortable but they are familiar, and our brain slips into unconscious long-term memory. In this old familiar rut, it goes into action (inaction) with hardly any conscious effort.

Please Note: The soul does not understand pretend or make-believe. That is why a true dream never dies.

Belief must match the desire. Measure your belief in you. Measure your belief in your purpose. Nothing is ever accomplished alone. Measure your belief in others and God. Assume good intentions. Expect the best or better.

When doubt arises, as Tim-the-Toolman-Taylor says, "Back the trolley up!" There are thoughts that may need to be kicked off. There are ineffective behaviors to be left behind. There are emotions to be felt and released. There are also ideas, attitudes, and abilities that are rushing to catch up. Back up so they can hop on board.

The action is a natural byproduct of desire fertilized by belief. Once the thinking neurons are in place, the body jump-starts and is raring to go. The proof is in practice. Employ the power of spaced repetition.

Empowerment comes to us one bite at a time. It starts off as information, nurtured by understanding and application that grows into belief, that leads to practice that produces an outcome.

How do you eat an elephant? "One bite at a time." Sure, it's one bite at a time - but it's more than that. It's one bite at a time with space for digestion and elimination. One bite at a time shared in the community; a community that gives new recipes and additive spices.

Caution: Since it is human nature to present self in the best light, we can easily lie to ourselves - to self-delude. Pay attention to feedback - internal and external. Whether one leans to the light side or shadow side of life depends largely on our motivation. Overt actions are subtle indicators of obscured attitudes. Self-evaluate not only actions but also the motive behind the actions.

CHAPTER 6

THE RELATIONSHIP BETWEEN COURAGE AND WEALTH

Courage is needed if you are to get the most from life. This trait is developed much like a physical muscle. It can be strengthened through consistent training and in the decisions you make within your daily life. Courage is a psychological muscle that helps you face life's challenges and develop resilience to hardship. Here are 10 strategies to build your courage so that you become your best self and to endure the trials of life:

1. Complete One Thing Outside Of Your Comfort Zone Every Day. Build up your courage step by step. This goal can be both big and small. Some examples may include driving to work a different route or signing up for a public speaking course. The point is to do things that promote growth and positive risk. Push yourself a little more every day and your courage will grow. This practice may be scary at first, but simply taking an action is the first step in building courage.

As you try bigger and greater challenges, you will notice that you are accomplishing things far beyond what you ever thought you could.

2. Prepare Yourself Ahead Of Time. You cannot always schedule the challenges of your life, but you can prepare yourself before such an event occurs. Get yourself in physical shape. If you had to run to get help for someone you care about; could you do it? If you had to pull someone from a car accident; do you have the strength to do so? Make physical exercise a regular part of your routine. Be persistent. The difference between an amateur and a professional is that the professional spends twenty more minutes for practice while an amateur stops at five minutes of practice.

3. Train Your Mind. When push comes to shove, the mind will be the key to getting you through whatever challenge you face. You must learn to believe in yourself. You must develop that habit of building yourself up through positive affirmation. Use "I Can" and "I Will" language instead of weaker statements like "I'll try" or "I may." Tell yourself that you are someone who makes things happen.

4. Your Courage Will Grow According To Your Desire. If you don't have a desire to develop courage, then you won't. Sometimes the best way to get motivated to develop courage is to consider what will happen if you don't. Think of all the missed opportunities. How will your career and relationships be negatively impacted? How will you feel about yourself? On the flip side, ask yourself what is the best

thing that could happen if you do take a positive risk. What if you ask your boss for that raise? What if you made a full commitment to your spouse and put your whole heart into the marriage?

5. Stay Away From People Who Have Stinking Thinking. Misery loves company. If your friends and family are keeping you from excelling in your life's best interest then maybe you need to distance yourself from them to some degree. A full separation may not be needed, but you do need to at least consider setting better boundaries in how you spend your time with them. The secret is not to let their negativity rub off on you. If you're not careful, their influence will define you in a very limiting way.

6. Be Original. Don't be afraid to go first. Think outside the box. Speak up with your twist as to how things could be done. Perhaps you know of a way to do old things in a new way. Too many people these days hide in the safety of sheepishness. Even if they have a great idea; they are afraid to come forth with it because of the possible ridicule and rejection from others. It is true that if you never try then, you'll never fail but then you'll never know victory or defeat either. These are the seeds of greatness. You must learn to overcome the fear of what others think of you and your ideas. Think of all the advances that have developed over the past twenty years because someone had the courage to be original.

7. Hold Onto Your Core Values. Moral courage has the determination to follow what you believe to be right

regardless of the cost to yourself or the disapproval of others. People of courage have strong core values, and they keep these core beliefs in mind every time they make a decision. When you make a decision, consider how it may affect your ability to look yourself in the mirror. Consider if your decision will hurt other people. Practice what you preach. Do not compromise on your values even when it's more convenient or to save your skin.

8. Develop The Art Of Being Poised. Courage is not boastful. People who demonstrate courage let their accomplishments speak for themselves. Most heroes do not see themselves as such. They believe an action needed to be taken and they did what was necessary.

9. Don't Psych Yourself Out. Remember the acronym, FEAR. False Evidence Appearing Real. Do not let your fears become any bigger than you have to. Your imagination can either be your greatest asset or your biggest enemy.

10. Read Books and Watch Movies with Tales of Courage. These serve as powerful examples that can inspire you. I love movies in which the underdog rises to the demand placed before him. These stories can point you in the direction of how to carry yourself as you seek to be a person of courage. I have often thought "How would Braveheart carry himself in a situation like this? Instead of having to spend a lot of time pondering my challenge; all I had to do was consider the example set by the character from the book or the movie that had inspired me.

CHAPTER 7

SUCCESS FACTORS

If you want to be successful in life, it is vital to know the various types of success factors that can help you achieve your goals. If you are aware of them and keep doing them all, you will be able to achieve just about anything you want in life.

One of the most vital success factors you should always consider using is time management. As you know, it is quite impossible to turn back the clock. Once you've done something, it is difficult to reverse the doing. If you know how to manage your time it becomes easy for you to complete whatever that is important for the day. Time management also gives you more time to relax and enjoy your life. Start by looking at the hours in the day and set your priorities to the tasks that need to be completed. Don't try to do everything on one day. This will lead to discouragement. I keep a to-do list in my office and prioritize it everyday. Because things change and, adjustments need to be made. The one thing I always do is to make time for family and friends because they are my priority. Make your to-do list achievable, and you will be quite surprised how the to do, becomes done.

Another one of the vital success factors is learning to become disciplined. However, this aspect is not an easy one and cannot be followed by everybody. Many people have great difficulty being disciplined for many personal reasons, and they have trouble focusing on one thing at a time. However, if you want to open up a business, you must make sure that you have this code of behavior in your arsenal. If you don't have, there is a great tendency that you will meet failure before you can taste the fruits of success. As discipline is one of the most important success factors, you need to force yourself to insert this quality in you if you don't have it yet. Discipline has been aptly described as " the bridge between goals and accomplishment." You need to learn to finish jobs, not get distracted and focus on the task at hand. Stay with it, in other words.

Some people might say that being a hardworking individual means you will be rewarded handsomely since you are incorporating one of the success factors into your life. However, this is only true up to a certain extent. If you want to achieve success, working smart should be one of the next success factors to consider. When you work the smart way, you can generate wealth and prosperity more easily because you are not devoting your whole energy, but rather you are finding ways to simplify the things you do. If you have a large task that needs to be completed, try to break it down into smaller tasks. Incorporate some help when you can. I once had a huge spreadsheet which required manual entry of hundreds of records. I asked my niece if she would like to earn a little cash to do the job. She jumped at the opportunity and saved hours of monotonous work which freed up my time for more important things.

Keep in mind that being goal oriented is also another one of the success factors to consider. When setting your goals, make sure that they are within your capacity to reach. If it seems like an impossible mission, you won't be motivated because you already know that you will meet a dead-end no matter what type of success factors you utilize into achieving the goals. It is also important to set a deadline or a specific timeframe to your goals so that you won't waste too much time dreaming rather than working. Be very specific when setting your goals. This will help you achieve them.

Having the right attitude should be included in the list of success factors as well. If you always tend to make excuses, you won't go far in whatever you set out to do. When you are an entrepreneur, and there is a problem in your business, you need to find a solution to your problem and not merely give up. If you can rise in the middle of the most critical situation, this means you have the right attitude. A good attitude is a "can do" attitude. You will certainly achieve success eventually when you are committed and don't give up when you encounter a setback. All in all, when you have incorporated these essential success factors into your life, it becomes easier for you to move forward and transform all of your dreams into reality.

They Understand the Magic of Goals

When a person sets goals for personal success, the achievement of those goals depends greatly on the goal-setting tactics that are used to set the original goals. People often set huge goals with huge rewards at the end of the journey. Nevertheless, this goal setting choices make success hard to obtain. When it comes to the personal success of goal setting, each personal needs to think big, aim small and celebrate every success for what it is worth, a success.

When choosing personal goal setting as the method to your end goal, there are a few tips that you can follow to increase your chance of success. Following the goal setting for the duration of your journey will increase the chances that life, no matter how twisted and turned it may become, will not sabotage your goal setting achievements.

Aim big, measure small. Goal setting needs to be realistic. If you are out to lose 100 pounds, the goal of one hundred pounds is too large. You need to make the goal setting task a smaller part of the whole. Ten pounds steps toward the larger end goals are easier to achieve and thus easier to maintain. In addition, the celebration from reaching each of the goal setting milestones can be celebrated and used a motivation for that next small step of goal setting success.

Reward yourself often. Along the same lines as setting small personal success, goals are rewarding yourself for those goals. On the same topic of weight loss, every time you lose those ten pounds, gives something back to you! This is the purpose of goal setting for success. Reaching the goals means patting yourself on the back and preparing for the next goal. Try rewarding yourself with something totally unrelated to the goal. Weight loss, for instance, should not be rewarded with beauty regimes. Nevertheless, something more tangible, like a stone in the garden or a new picture on the wall.

Take the help you need. Pride in goal setting is often the hamper to our success. When we need help achieving our goals, there are often many people around us willing to give that help, but the prideful creatures we are, we aim at accomplishing that goal setting success all by ourselves. A goal that is reached, is a success no matter if you have helped or not!

Be ready to revise. Life comes at you quick and with life comes the chance of a roller coaster ride. We need to revise our methods of goal setting at every turn in the road if that is what is needed to make the success real. Achievement and success are not measured by the goal, but by the ability to continue, moving forward despite the troubles and hindrances to our goal setting life may create.

Do not fret the missed goals. Not every goal will be met and that is just the way it should be. If goal setting always ended in success, there would be no need to do anything else in life except set goals. There will be ups and down along the path and goal setting simply allows you to stay focused on the bigger picture of overall success, even if there are stumbles.

Taking your time and setting goals that are achievable will make the difference in goal setting for personal success. It is the goals we set in our lives that make us drive for more and strive for the best. Goal setting needs to be realistic and open to change. Moreover, when goals setting works and those success goals are reached, celebrate and reward yourself.

Everybody would like to improve himself or herself in some way. However, the sad truth is that most people try for a little bit and then give up. It is no secret that only about ten percent of people who purchase personal development books and courses actually get through the whole book or course. And with so many new systems coming out every year, you would think people would be getting better. But most people do not think they are. The good news is that it is no nearly as difficult as you think to improve yourself in real ways.

First of all, you need to begin. You cannot achieve anything if you do not start. When should you start? However, when people think of starting a Development Plan, they imagine making huge strides right out of the gate. It is much easier to take baby steps. Inch by inch, life's a cinch. Just commit yourself to making small progress each day, and you will get there in no time.

Another mistake people make is to set huge goals that are hard to achieve on their own. Sure, having huge, larger than life goals are essential, but you have to take the time to break them down into small chunks. How do you eat an elephant? One bite at time. If you want to lose one hundred pounds in a year, that comes out to just under two pounds per week. Losing two pounds in a week is a much easier goal to think of than losing a hundred pounds in a year.

Of course, you will not hit your short-term goals all the time. Figure two steps forward, and one-step back, and you are doing just fine. So maybe shift your target of a hundred pounds to a year and a half. After all, as soon as you achieve that goal, you are going to want to set and achieve another one. No sense in making life hard and frustrating. Just go at slow enough pace so it is easy to do, and just enough to measure progress every couple weeks.

No matter what kind of goal you are going after, you are going to need to read information and learn things about it. Spend at least an hour every couple weeks researching your goal and finding different ways to achieve it. Of course, after you start to notice some small progress, you will be super motivated to learn more, so you will likely be spending a lot more than an hour a week.

The best thing you can do is tell as many people as you can about your goal. That way, you will feel accountable. Studies have shown that people who tell their friends and family they are going to quit smoking by a certain day have a much larger success rate than people who try to quit on their own without telling anybody.

Following these simple steps can really help you to achieve almost any goal. Just pick one that fires you up, break it down into small chunks, and take small steps every day in the direction of your goal. You will get there before you know it.

Network marketers must set goals. Period. Many I have found, however, have no clue as to how to set viable goals to assure the success of their network marketing business.

How often have you found yourself saying something like, "I'd like a huge down line and a beach house in Spain," or, "I want to be the same size I was in high school?" How many times have you actually mapped out what it would take to make those things happen?

Do not mistake wishing or wanting for goal-setting. Simply desiring your network marketing business to take off so you can quit your job will not bring it much closer to becoming reality. Setting a goal to achieve a specific end, however, is a completely different story.

Your goals must be meaningful to you. This should go without saying, but every day I see people trying to achieve goals set for them by others. A goal set for you by your employer or spouse is not really a goal at all.

To be effective, your goals must be specific. "I want to make a lot of money," is not a goal. You must state how much you will accomplish, and by what date, you will have this done. "I want to earn $5,000 a month in residual income by August 31 of this year," is a valid goal.

For goals to be specific, you must write them down. Many insist using paper and pen, but I find typing mine on my computer works just fine. That way, I can continually edit and update them.

Written goals provide direction to your activities, kind of like a road map. With so much information out there, it is sometimes difficult to know which steps to take and when. By reviewing your written goals, you get a better sense of what needs to be done right now.

When writing goals, begin with brainstorming. This means dreaming. Write down, uncensored, everything you would like to have in your life, from now until the end of your life. Do not even think about it. Just write.

When you finish this, make another list of goals. Limit this to things you want to accomplish in the next twelve months. Make sure these goals mesh with your longer term goals.

The next step is very important. In order for goals to be realized, a price must be paid. It is like in physics, the whole "for every action there exists an equal and opposite reaction" thing. Nothing is free.

Your task, then, is to erase those goals you are not willing to pay the price for. For instance, if your goal is to live in Southern France, but your mate wants to live close to family, are you willing to do what it takes to achieve that goal? If not, it is not doable, and is not a viable goal.

Once you have your short and long-term goals written down, you must break them down into smaller, more manageable chunks. For example, if it is your goal to recruit fifty new downline members in twelve months, how many will you need to recruit in 90 days?

What will you need to do in those 90 days to make that happen? What do you need to do next week? Tomorrow? Right now? Make a list of activities you simply must do to attain these goals. This keeps it real.

Which brings me to another point. To be challenging and motivating, your goals must be perceived as attainable. I have seen people set some lofty goals, only to feel an overwhelming sense of failure when they could not achieve them. Small, even baby steps sometimes are necessary to build confidence.

Rewrite your goals every 3 months or so. If you are like me, your goals are constantly changing to some degree. Rewriting helps keep them, and you, focused on what you really want and are striving for.

Written goals help you end up where you want to be, kind of like a boat with oars, or even a motor and a rudder. Contrast that with the majority of people who, it seems, float aimlessly and have no clue where they will end up.

Everyone has a goal or a dream. It is that which motivates a person to keep moving forward and see it to completion. It could be a simple goal, such as losing some weight, or applying for your dream job. It could be something bigger, like opening your dream business, or finally purchasing your first home. Whatever it is, it should encourage you to go beyond what you would normally expect from yourself.

However, if you are like most people, you will experience different levels of fear and nervousness. It is that butterfly-in-the-stomach feeling you get - when your heart beats faster, your teeth chatter, you sweat buckets and experience sleepless nights.

These are actually normal feelings brought about by the uncertainty of possible results. The thought of plunging into unchartered waters does seem daunting, and quite nerve-wracking.

However, if these feelings make you freeze with fright and make you give up on a goal, then it becomes an abnormal fear. Self-doubt is totally detrimental to one's growth as a person. Unusual fear will result to non-action, and you end up a failure - even before you start.

How does one overcome fear and self-doubt? Here are a few steps you must take in order to shake it off from your life.

Make a commitment to yourself. One of the best ways you can use to yourself motivate is to commit to the fulfillment of your goal. Make the decision to see it through. There will be obstacles, but with dedication and a positive mindset, you will see your goal coming to fruition, and your self-doubt melting right before you. Stop worrying about things that might happen. Instead, plant the seed of hope and resolve inside you - because these will be the fuel to light up that fire of determination which you need to achieve your goals. Fulfill the commitment you made to yourself, because no one else will do it for you.

Separate yourself from your fears. Whether you like it or not, fear and self-doubt will always come a-knocking on your door. It's like the devil, tempting those who have the most faith. Although some fears are not entirely baseless, remember that you are given talents to counteract them. Always keep in mind that fear is just an emotion - which means, it has no business messing with your life.

Change your attitude about failure. Rather than view failure as obstacles, see them lessons. Admit it - not all your endeavors will go as planned and not all plans will succeed. If it were so easy to be successful, then there wouldn't really be a big deal about success. People will not try so hard, and no one will push themselves beyond their limits. Change your view about failure - look at them as bit and pieces of life lessons that help you grow stronger with every incidence.

Build up your confidence. Take a step back and assess yourself - what are your strengths? What are the things you are better at when compared to others? Oftentimes, you don't realize how lucky you are compared to others - and viewing your life from a different perspective opens your mind to possibilities which you don't know you were capable of reaching. Empower yourself by thinking of what it is in you that makes you above par. Use these attributes to trample on fear and self-doubt. Be confident, and believe then you are capable!

The only way to get rid of doubt is by keeping reality in perspective. People are all made of the same fiber - some are stronger, while others break when faced with challenges. Don't be part of the broken. Instead, be a believer - and show them that you, too, can be successful in whatever you want to do. Remember, only you and you alone can do this - no one can do it for you.

Dealing with Stressful Situations

Some people nowadays have become very busy with their work which is why a recent study says that the majority of persons are becoming stressed. Stress is something that might take your energy which would make a person feel tired and restless. That's why it is vital that you find out what could help combat stress.

One of the best ways to do this is by drinking coffee since it has caffeine. Just in case you are looking for the perfect coffee machine, then have a look at what the Keurig single cup coffee maker and the Senseo Supreme has to offer. But of course, besides from coffee, there are various other means to be alert at work.

To find out much more about what can de-stress you after a tiring day, then here are some ideas that work:

Caffeine

First thing on the list as mentioned would be receiving a daily amount of caffeine. This is an excellent way to combat stress due to the fact coffee gives that fresh aroma which could help someone relax. It is also a fantastic solution for people who feel sleepy. Coffee is a regarded antioxidant so should you want to cleanse, then be sure to have your day-to-day dose of caffeine.

Enjoyable Massage

Another excellent way that could also help a person de-stress is by having a comforting body massage while having your lunch break. Getting a massage would support people loosen up their tensed muscles and they could also clear their minds.

Exercise

Exercises are another good way to fight stress. For people with a gym within your office, it would not hurt to step on the treadmill to help you relax. If you feel you typically get distressed, try doing a bit of workout in the morning so it would contribute to improving your day.

Online Games

This is also one of the things that folks do. There are lots of online games from which to choose and it can certainly help you to de-stress since getting this done would help people use their minds along with their imaginations. In recent times, plenty of games online is available which is the reason it's also considered as a popular way of passing the time. This can be best if you have a video game room inside your office, so you spend time playing video games throughout your break.

Flower Power

Finally, you might like to buy flowers because it helps brighten the atmosphere and it is a very simple means of de-stressing one's self. Should you have flowers on your desk, then you can stare at it and it can certainly relax.

Stress is one of the principal causes of sleeping problems, so you may find that dealing with your stress may often be exactly the trick you need to assist you to deal with sleeping disorders. Those who are not sleeping can on occasion attribute their sleeplessness to all kinds of factors, yet stress is often the primary reason why you're having problems sleeping. Stress causes adrenaline to be produced, and excitement wakes you up at times you ought to be sleeping.

If you are trying to sleep but can't, here are some steps to take to tackle your stress-based sleep difficulty:

Relax more in the evening - The night is usually a very stressful time for those with little kids, as well as for individuals who have to spend a lot of time sitting in traffic. It's crucial that you can calm down as much as possible in the evening, as this will guarantee your body can manage to relax and eliminate the stress of the day. Take the time to relax in your most comfortable chair and watch a movie in the evening, or read a great novel. Make sure to keep away from whatever is likely to cause you to be active through the night since that will make the sleep problem to intensify.

Exercise early in the AM - If you are used to working out at night, chances are the subsequent stress will add to your sleeplessness. Exercising in the morning can help you to reduce your stress levels, as the hormone flow within your system as the result of exercise may make it possible to relax your body the entire day. Additionally, it can cause you to be more fatigued in the evening, and all this can deal with your sleeping problems properly. It's best to avoid exercising after 7 or 8 PM, because your body will still be loaded with adrenaline when time to going to sleep.

Engage in something non-stressful later in the day -Stress frequently stimulates your body to race, and you could realize that your sleeping problem is the result of a mind that's too packed with emotions, anxieties, and concerns. If you like to let your brain wind down - which will lead to your body relaxing - it's essential to do things which call for very little mental effort. Board games are quite soothing, and puzzles can help you to put your active mind on hold.

Claim your 'me' time - Allowing yourself some time alone on the weekend can do wonders to solve your sleeping problems, as you will be able to unwind and take it easy after a long full week. Staying up late on Fridays and Saturdays isn't always a problem, as you can sleep in the following day. Even so, it's best to try and keep your sleeping patterns regular, and thus you should go to sleep on weekend evenings as during the week. By taking time off during the weekend, you can take pleasure in soaking in the bath, go to the gym, do some sports, enjoy a good magazine, or relax in front of the TV. You need to spend at a minimum of a couple of hours engaged in leisurely and soothing activities.

Do What They Love

Everyone seems to be born with different skills and talents. Some are great drawers and artists while others are naturally good with mathematics and numbers. Some have gifts apropos music while others are athletic. How does one know what your abilities and abilities are? The solution to that's sometimes finding out what you are good at and what you like doing. More times than not they're one and the same thing.

For somebody like Wayne Gretzky the solution to this was playing hockey while for somebody like John Kennedy it was to be a leader.

You've just got to follow your calling and then have the bravery to follow your dreams. For somebody it could be a plumber while for some other person it can be being a designer and planning buildings for which people can live.

People can go thru their full life without discovering the answer to this question. They meander from one thing to the subsequent simply making an attempt to untangle this. This is how you get some individuals that study medication for 6 years and following this they do something else. Then you have others who do law for approximately the same quantity of time and then begin working as counsel only to realise that they do not like it and it's not for them.

It is important that you aren't pressured into something over another. Certain vocations are preferred as they are higher earning but it is better to do something you enjoy and like doing. No amount of money can compensate for doing something which you don't enjoy. You are only going to feel resentful and upset. Life is too short to be in this position.

You have to have the bravery to follow your dreams and do whatever it is your heart tells you. It'd mean being a gardener, being a bingo player or being a baker. You may need to become a paparazzo or a dancer. There is not any wrong or right answer. Just what you like doing.

It's your life and you're the one who has to live it. No point in doing things for folks which will be to the detriment of yourself. You want to worry yourself less with what other folks think and make your own feelings the no 1 concern. Or you are always going to feel upset and empty within.

Many people do something only because their parents want them to do it. They are trying to follow their parent's wishes and not want to disappoint them. It could be a family business and they are being looked to like the person to carry it on. This is a nice idea but if it isn't for you, you need to let the people in your family know. If you don't both of you are going to suffer in the long run. It might be short term pain but it's the best for the long run.

CHAPTER 8

FINANCIAL PLANNING AND DEBT MANAGEMENT

There are some basic needs we all have as individuals that need to be met. At the top of the list are the needs necessary for survival - food, clothing, shelter. These basic needs can be met with ease when one has financial prosperity to meet those needs.

The focus is to be able to meet our daily needs. Jesus never went around with a lot of money (although he did have a treasurer. Broke people don't need treasurers). He also knew that he would be able to meet every need that arose because he walked in financial prosperity. He knew how to meet needs once they arose.

Here are some ideas on what it means to walk in financial prosperity;

1. Knowing that you can meet every need that comes up - there are always enough resources to meet current needs. The fallacy is when we look at a need and believe there is no

provision. In America, we waste a ton of food each day. People eat at a restaurant and leave plenty of food on their plates. It's amazing how those who have resources tend to waste more than those who don't.

2. Knowing that you have more than you will ever need at your disposal - an abundance mentality is necessary to walk in financial prosperity. This mentality will create within us the assurance that we have all that we need whenever we need it. All we have to do is learn how to tap into this abundance which is all around us.

3. Never thinking you are in lack but only in abundance - it is very hard to think "I have abundant resources at my disposal." That is exactly what we must think to achieve our goals. As a man thinks, so shall he become. We have to think that we can meet every need at every occasion if we hope to live that way.

4. Never speaking lack but talking abundance - just like we have to think abundance, we have to speak it as well. Negative talk does not give us positive results. What you want to see happen in your life you must be willing to say it. The focus has to be on becoming what we envision and that includes being bold enough to say what we mean and mean what we say.

There are many ways to go about creating prosperity. All these various methods do have one concept that ties them all together, though, which is that you need to develop a consciousness of prosperity.

You must have the proper thinking process in place as you go about creating prosperity. This way of thinking is one where you go out of your way to avoid paying interest charges. You will save first and buy the big screen TV second. When you do buy that big screen TV, it will be with cash you've saved to avoid financing it. The cash you use for your big screen TV will be more than your emergency fund and retirement savings.

Do you see how this financial prosperity mindset is quite different from the mindset of most people you know you are constantly struggling to get out of debt? Do you see how different it is than the mindset they try to sell you on TV or in other various forms of advertising?

Is this harder to do than to just go crazy charging up credit cards and department store accounts like most people? Yes, it is. But, if you desire to attain financial prosperity to live a life of financial success, it's necessary to live by this prosperity consciousness.

That being said, you may be wondering what activities you should be utilizing to attain true financial prosperity. You could do one or more of the following: invest in rental real estate properties, invest into retirement accounts such as IRA's, Roth IRA's, 401(k)'s, Self Employed IRA's, etc, invest in stocks and bonds, invest in option trading, invest in businesses, invest into an emergency account until you have 3 to 6 to 12 months income saved, start a home business (website, network marketing, etc.).

Now, not all of these activities are right for everyone. Some of them require proper training and knowledge to do well. However, if you're not willing to invest some time and energy into learning the specifics of some of these activities that help create prosperity for you, as well as helping when it comes to getting out of debt, financial abundance will elude you.

What if you possess the prosperity consciousness already discussed but just lack the financial resources to build that emergency fund or contribute toward that Roth IRA?

If you're serious about financial prosperity, then you may want to see what you can do to increase your income. You've got to fight and claw to find a way to do this. Maybe you need to take a second job to find the seed money for your home business.

You may be closer to creating prosperity than you think. Nowadays, you could set up a simple website that centers around a talent or passion that you have. Rather than thousands or millions, the money needed to get a website started is only a few hundred dollars.

Creating financial prosperity just takes the right mindset, a prosperity consciousness, and the patience to watch your wealth slowly grow. You'll realize financial abundance once you've worked toward your plan for some years.

Billionaire Prioritize their Expenditure

Except for the rich, we all need to watch our spending. Money management is a very simple concept; spend less than we earn!

Easy to say, but difficult to do especially at various stages of our lives.

When we are young we are like a growing business; we need to invest in homes, our families and other things for getting established. This makes it almost impossible to spend less than we earn, so it is necessary to use debt to build our lives. It is also necessary to establish priorities for what we buy with cash or debt.

If we prepare a budget early on it will help us get control of our necessities very quickly. If we are honest, we discover that it doesn't take a lot of income just to survive. Then we need to focus on making enough money to pay for them and have some money left over, or profit as a business would call it. Our profit should be invested in a backup fund and other things we need to build our lives and live free. This is a very over-simplified financial model, but it is a very fundamental one.

Prioritizing our expenditures that are not necessities is where we often get into trouble. Over spending results in high credit card balances that are difficult to be free of and only makes it more difficult for us to invest in the things we want, such as a house and improved living standards.

So, how do we establish priorities on how we use our discretionary cash? There are many resources for guiding us in making these decisions, but I have another way to look at it. We should prioritize our discretionary spending on what will make us happy!

My definition of happiness it to have inner peace, another's centered purpose, and to make a living that gives us freedom. If we have credit cards that are over extended, we will worry and have stress that inhibits our inner peace. If we focus too much on just ourselves, we will only see tons of things we want for self-fulfillment. We may also fall in to envying others for what they have and seek to get those things for ourselves. We can become greedy, even if we are not wealthy. We often fall into a "pity party" when we get too self-centered and believe we are "victims" as we are not paid enough, and don't have as much money as we deserve. This will only take us down and destroy our inner peace.

If we learn to be thankful for what we have and understand how much others don't have, our attitude can change. We can even consider using some of our discretionary money to help others.

So our spending priorities should be based on a higher level, that of having real happiness; inner peace, purpose and freedom that comes from controlling our debt. Some would call this avoiding instant gratification; I call it seeking total happiness.

With each expenditure we make we should ask ourselves the simple question, will this make us happy?

Billionaire have a Debt Management Plan

Many people have experienced the overwhelming pile of debt that makes it difficult to get ahead. This is one of the major things in life that causes tension in folks everyday life. When not addressed, debt issues can cause medical problems as well as problems in relationships within the family. There are some steps that can be taken to help with this type of issue.

This section will cover some areas of debt management and reduction. You need to know how to handle debt, what debt management is and how to obtain help and why help is important. The information will give some knowledge about debt management plans. This will assist you in your journey as well as for those that you may know that are experiencing similar issues regarding their financial problems.

A debt management plan arises from allowing financial debt experts access to your financial details and, having studied the difficulties you find yourself in due to mounting debt; they produce a plan which allows you to pay off your creditors. Where a debt management plan differs from you trying to deal with an escalating situation of debt yourself, is that the debt management company contacts your creditors and strikes a deal with them about how much you have to pay back per month to them. Most creditors not surprisingly, are happy to deal with debt management companies, as they know that with a debt management company involved, they have a better chance of getting money from a debtor on a monthly basis, albeit at a possibly reduced rate.

Another benefit of using a debt management plan is that once the company begins the process of negotiating with your creditors, the pressure of dealing with these companies is greatly reduced. Those telephone calls will stop as well as those threatening letters. The company that you owe money to will communicate with your debt management professional. The worry and stress will soon begin to dissipate.

Also when you put a debt management plan into place, the interest being charged and other charges get frozen, so that your financial debt does not escalate out of control any further. You simply pay an amount that you can afford, as judged by the debt management company and a time scale is worked out whereby it is estimated that the debt will be cleared.

There are multiple ways of obtaining a debt management plan, and a financial adviser that is willing to help you. To ensure, however, that you are well taken care of and that your interests are being considered first and foremost, it is advisable to work with a financial institution that has a proven success rate for similar cases. An excellent place to begin your research on such institutions is at Chase Saunders. Their website is an excellent resource that will provide you will important and useful information about the programs and plans that they offer their valued customers. Begin your research today, and discover how to change your life, or the life of a friend of family member, for the better.

It is becoming a difficult task to handle finances day by day. The time is changing at a fast pace. Today, People need to acquire a basic knowledge of their earning and spending. People rarely understand the importance of it in their new modern life. And that is why; people create a huge mountain of debt. It takes understanding to make a right decision at the time of financial crisis. Whether it is a small or medium-sized debt, it has to be cleared as soon as it can be. There are many plans to implement for clearing any debt. If you are unable to repay your payments, then you can apply for this plan. As, the Debt management plan is one of the best ways, which works properly for you. This plan is about a contract between the debtor and the creditor to manage all your repayments into a single refund.

It is a casual agreement between a debtor and creditor. A Debtor gets a relief because of reduced repayments for a fixed period. The time depends on your means to afford your refunds. So, it gives you the ability to retain your financial control.

People can implement this plan by a licensed debt management company. So, you would be having correct operations while pursuing this plan. The important thing is for a company to enroll you in this plan. That's your debts relief plan UK which should be an unsecured. It means your loan has to be without any security. It is because then, the company can work in the best manner to help you well. It is a basic requirement to apply to the debt management plan.

As per the changing times, you need to be an alert to managing your income as well as your expenses. Sometimes, it is not possible to take care of small expenses, however; they can turn into huge costs. These costs could be the reason for taking a loan and your debts. So, try to avoid your unnecessary expenses and you would be able to preserve a good amount of money.

However, debt management seems a competent option to handle your multiple debts with ease. Many debt companies are managing these cases of debts, and they will offer you proper advice on this matter.

Debt management is an appropriate solution for the debtor who is looking for settling his debt. By this plan, you would be assured and motivated to pay off your repayments to your creditors. Reduced refunds provide you a helping hand to have manageable finances as well.

Benefits of Debt Management

Debt management plans are designed especially for those struggling to meet escalating debt repayments. By getting in touch with your creditors, the debt management company will request that your payments will be lowered to an affordable monthly rate.

If you're considering a debt management plan, you need to know all the details of what it will entail. Here, we have put together a list of the advantages of taking out a debt management plan:

Free financial consultation

You can receive a free financial consultation where the debt management company will discuss your financial situation in detail to find which solution is the most suitable for you.

Reduce your debts in an affordable way

With the help of a debt management company, you will be able to move multiple debts into manageable and affordable payments.

With your consent, the payment can be set on a specific date each month, most suitable to you.

Freeze your interest and charges

Although this isn't guaranteed with all debt management plans, it is possible to set a repayment plan that isn't subject to change, either interest or non-payment charges. With this in place, you will be able to maintain your payments without the risk of facing further charges on top of your set schedule.

You no longer deal with creditors

Once you have decided to take a debt management plan, you won't have to deal with any of your creditors. The debt management company will do all the running for you and make all your inquiries to the creditors. They will even write and post all the letters to the creditors - making your role much easier.

Payment plan that you can stick to

Every month you will only have one simple payment to one creditor - the debt management company. This will make keeping up with your payments a lot easier as you won't have to juggle different payment dates, rising charges and multiple creditors.

Frequent re-evaluation of your payment plan

Many debt management companies can set up a re-evaluation program, if you struggle to make the new payments. You can arrange for a meeting every 6 months to re-assess the payment plan and ensure you're able to meet each payment. If not, you can arrange to change or reduce your monthly repayments, with permission of course.

One payment a month

With only one payment required every month, you'll find it far easier to maintain your payments. Struggling to keep your mounting debts in order will be a thing of the past - the debt management plan will do all of the hard work for you.

Debt Prioritization by Billionaires

The debts of some people have increased along with the extreme use of credit cards, that some debts are even amounting to a figure they can barely afford. What you need to know are effective ways to get out of debt because even if you throw out your bills, cut your credit cards or hide them to the deepest part of your drawer, the debt would not go away.

You could decrease if not eliminate your accumulating debts if you read on the ways and tips that I have listed below. As you read along, part those you can do and will work for you from those things that could work for you and start working on them right away.

Stop getting new debt

The first and most rational thing that you need to do to stop accumulating your debts is to stop acquiring new debts. One of the basis, why you lose control of your debt, is because you keep on adding to it, so you should stop using your credit cards to finance anything.

You do not need your credit card to live and they only serve as a trap if you are already in debt. It will not be easy to eliminate credit cards from your life, but in the end, you would realize that it was a relief to let go of them.

Prioritize your debts

Debts with the highest interest should be paid first because it tends to drain off money that you could be using for something else, and this is one financial rule you should keep in mind.

It is better to pay off your debts one at a time, starting with the smaller amounts first to push you to keep up your good work once it gives you the sense of accomplishment.

Record all your spending

Writing down all the expenses that you did in a week can make you see where you can cut down your spending. You can avoid accruing your debts by actually knowing where you spend your money on.

Get a second occupation

You could pay off your debts, starting with those who have the highest interests first with the extra cash that you would be earning from your second job. You would know that you have paid your debts in no time when you tackle them one by one.

Cutting down all your expenditures and luxuries may be at hard at first, but it might save you from bigger troubles in the future. By following the ways to get out of debt above, you could free yourself from financial miseries that have imprisoned you for so long.

When it seems that you have more debts than your hands can handle, then you need to learn the debt juggling trick called prioritizing. Prioritizing your debts is foundational to paying them off as quickly as possible. You have to become more skillful in knowing which bills get paid this month and which ones will have to wait. Prioritizing is the DIY method of debt management. It gives you a way to make more effective use of the money you are using to pay off debts by concentrating on retiring one debt at a time.

1. Do your paperwork first

Get accurate, up to date data on each of your debts. If you are not sure, contact your creditors to give you the information. Write down the interest rates, balances, and minimum monthly payments for each debt you have. Also, write out the terms and conditions of each debt. For example, some loans have prepayment penalties that make paying them off quickly less cost-effective.

2. Arrange them by the highest effective interest rate. Note: Interest payment on mortgages or student loans are less than the stated interest rate because interest on these loans is tax-deductible.

The effective rate is calculated by multiplying the stated interest rate by the difference between 1 and your income tax bracket as in the example below.

For 30% tax bracket, and a mortgage of 12% stated rate - Effective interest rate is $12 \times (1-0.3) = 8.4\%$

3. Work out how much of your monthly income you can afford to put towards clearing your debt. Use a tighter budget to help you to get more money in this debt-clearing account. Pay the minimum monthly payments on all your debts except for the one with the highest interest rate. Pay as much as you can above the minimum payment on the highest interest rate debt. Keep doing this until that debt is paid off then move to the next debt on the list.

All of us have limited incomes. And when our expenses begin to exceed the income that we are bringing in, we have to make choices. This involves prioritizing debt.

Before you can begin to prioritize your debts, you have to know what your debts are. The best way to do this is to take a piece of paper or a spreadsheet and start to list all of your debts. This includes things like your credit cards, rent, mortgage, car payments, utilities, tuition - everything.

Once you have them listed start to organize them by order of importance. The ones at the top of the list should be the ones that will impact your lives the most if you were not to pay them. If two debts are of equal importance, the one that should take priority is the one that is charging you the highest interest rate. By the time you complete this list, you will have a really good blueprint as to the order in which you should pay your bills.

Also, consider late fees in making your prioritization list. This is especially true with regards to credit card companies who have begun to charge exorbitant late fees. So, for example, if one credit card charges 12% with a twenty-five dollar late fee charge and a second card charges 10% but has a fifty dollar late fee charge, it might be better to prioritize the second card even though it has a lower interest rate. There are other things to consider as well. The important thing is that going through this process will force you to read the credit agreements on many of the debts that you have. You may be surprised to find what kind of liabilities you are subject to.

The best time to prioritize your debts is before you need to. Don't wait until your bills are starting to pile up on you before making your list. Doing this helps you a great deal even if you are not behind in your payments. It forces you to be aware of how much money you are spending. A large part of why many people find themselves deep in debt is that they lose a job or other source of income. But another large part of why people fall into debt is that they simply don't pay attention to the debts that are piling up. Before they know it, they owe too much to catch up. Keeping a prioritization list like this helps you to pay attention.

CHAPTER 9

WAYS BILLIONAIRES REDEMPTION FROM FINANCIAL CRISIS

There have been many companies and individuals who have suffered financially. This has caused a rise in the number of bankruptcies among individuals and small businesses. The sudden shift in the economic scenario has left many people with a lot of debts and no way to repay these loans.

Looming Financial Crisis

Fortunately, there are many organizations who are experts in Australian debt recovery, debt management, and expert negotiators who are helping people slowly sinking with too many debts and loans. The main culprit has been the easy availability of which has allowed people to take out loans and in many cases overextended themselves. When the credit crunch hit hard, they were just not in a position to repay the loan and the overdue interest. It is in this scenario that a debt mediator or negotiator helps by assessing your financial situation and then working out a plan to hold off your creditors. The most appropriate way would be to go in for a debt consolidation loan, which is a legal agreement set up between your creditors and yourself through the offices of a debt mediator.

Consolidating Debt Program

By making use of a debt consolidation loan, you will be able to get some relief from your creditors and also avoid declaring bankruptcy, which would affect your credit ratings immeasurably. Here, they consolidate or combine all your outstanding loans into one amount, which means that you have only one monthly repayment to be made. This loan is usually arranged through bad credit personal loan lenders who will consolidate all your debts into one single loan which will be negotiated for repayment at a much lower interest rate. This saves you a lot of tension, as the loan pays off your most serious and urgent creditors while ensuring others that there is hope that they will get their money back.

Future Financial Stability

Having decided that the only way to exit this financial mess is going through debt mediators; you will then have to fill in the necessary paperwork detailing the entire plus and minus points of your current financial status. This might include all your income sources, usual monthly expenses, and how much you pay as loan repayment; the list will also include the creditors and how much each is owed. After the application is reviewed and approved by one of the bad credit personal loan lenders, your debt consolidation loan will be sanctioned. The organization will usually allot a debt counselor who will guide you through this debt problem, till you reach some financial stability.

In the past, top countries in the world have witnessed several economic recessions. Their downfall also affects other countries, especially those that depend on them for the supply of goods and services. Just recently in 2008, America faced a similar situation, though the country is already making efforts to recover from it. If they don't employ the correct procedures, it is possible that they may witness the recession again. European countries are not exempted from this as countries such as Spain and Portugal are experiencing unfavorable economic situations. Greece is almost unable to pay its debts and Italy's story is also frustrating. If the right steps are not taken soon, these problems may even become worse. Hence, the EU and the American government are considering various bail-out plans and strategies for reforming their economies.

One of the indicators of recession is hyperinflation. Hyperinflation is a situation where the prices of goods and services rise to unreasonable levels. The situation is usually caused by currency debasement. This happens because currency's value depreciates and salary earners find it more difficult to buy products since they have risen higher in price. In most cases, people doing business usually cope better than salary earners because they can increase the prices of their goods and services. In fact, those in the middle class face more trouble because most of their earnings come from salaries and since their salaries are not high, they are unable to get what they want during hyperinflation. Another problem that the middle class may face is that their savings will depreciate by the time they make a withdrawal. Interest rates on deposits are low at this time, so people who have been saving in the bank for years will lose a lot of money.

Unfortunately, economic recession lasts several years and government strategies to effect reformation can take years before the results are seen. The government may also face a challenge from the population unable to believe in their policies even when sounding great. Some governments still make things worse by implementing the wrong policies. For instance, printing fiat currency in high amounts will make the economy worse because this can cause inflation.

When inflation is caused by too much money in the hands of people, printing more notes is simply a bad idea. Instead, a better strategy would be to reduce the money in people's hands by implementing reasonable programs. More so, the government can increase interest rates so that people will be encouraged to do business which in turn can cause economic recovery and growth.

When the economic recession is very severe, banks and the stock market do not perform well. In times like this, the people can react aggressively and cause anarchy. Survival measures such as hoarding water and staple foods increase and some people even look for defensive facilities such as guns to protect themselves if any alarm arises. In some other cases, the people may transfer their reserves to other countries where they feel their investment will be safe.

The recession is ugly and it's something you would not want to experience. It's necessary to pray that these problems will never occur. Apart from prayers, helping the government to implement the right policies is also important.

The financial crisis made many people tighten their purse strings and re-evaluate what was important as their mortgages, wages and stocks were all battered. Now that the markets are recovering people are beginning to spend once again, though still more carefully than before the crisis.

One of the main issues for every man in the financial crisis was housing valuation. Those with variable rate mortgages found themselves owing much more than what they paid for their houses, and many were unable to come up with the extra tens of thousands of dollars each year. But recent data shows that nationwide home prices are back down where they should be, in line with median household incomes.

Thinking of buying now that the market has calmed down? Find a mortgage financial advisor in your area to discuss what you are financially able to swing...that way, you know that you won't end up in foreclosure, as so many Americans have in the last few years.

There have also been many advances beyond housing. Corporations are once again turning profits. Much of this came at the expense of jobs in plants and stores, which helped to cause the crisis, but it also paved the way for recovery. And though no one wants to cheer for "the man," the fact that he is profiting means that we, the people, are making enough money to spend as we desire, not as life demands. Which is our next sign of solid recovery: consumer spending.

Consumer spending tightened during the recession in the face of layoffs, furloughs and the loss of benefits. But today consumers are spending. Some analysts complain that the extra expenditures come in the form of health care. Though health care costs are soaring, it is important to point out that dining, recreation and clothing sectors are also seeing a rise in profits. The important difference now from before the crisis is that consumers are saving.

Focus on What you can Control

My friend Michelle asks the wrong questions. The other day she wanted to go to the cellular store on a holiday. She called the store in the afternoon to make sure they were open and found out they would be closing early for the day - too late for her to get there and have time to pick out a new phone. Michelle then spent the next several minutes asking me questions such as, "Why do they close early? Why do they bother to open at all? If they're going to close soon, they might as well have stayed home. It's just 3 hours - what are they going to do with 3 hours? Why don't they just remain open for their regular workday?" And on and on.

Instead, she should be asking how she can fit a visit to the store into her schedule tomorrow, and how she can avoid having this happen in the future. And that got me to thinking: How often are we focusing on the things we cannot control, rather than those things we can control?

It's like the weather: Everyone talks about it, but no one does anything about it. Why? Obviously because we can't do anything about it. We can't control the weather, but we can certainly control where we live. Hate the snow of the north? Move south. Don't like the summer heat? Move to the coast.

It's the same way in your online business; if you simply focus on those things you can control and stop wasting time on the things you cannot control, you will be happier and more productive.

You cannot control time, but you can control what you do with your time.

You cannot control the customer service given to your customers by affiliate product owners, but you can control which products you promote, and thereby increase the odds of your customers getting great service, and continuing to click your links and buy based on your recommendations.

You cannot control the economy, but you can control how you earn and invest your money.

You cannot control what your competitors do, but you can control your own business and thus your own destiny.

You cannot always control what happens in life, but you can control how you react to what happens.

Getting what you want out of life is all about controlling what you can control, and using it to your own advantage.

You control your life. You control whether you're doing the things you're doing out of obligation or out of desire. You control your destiny.

Forget the things you cannot control and focus on those things that are within your power to control. You'll find you have less stress and more success.

Many new currency traders just do not know and understand the fact that risk analysis and money management is important in currency trading. Many think why money management has to be so annoying when they hear the word money management. It's just this kind of behavior that gets average novice trader into trouble. Why is money management so annoying?

Getting into a trade is thrill enough in itself at first glance. This is what most of the novice traders do in fact think that the currency market will do exactly what you want it to do, and you will end up with a trade that can make you a lot of money. You seduce yourself into thinking that once you enter the business, it will be hunky dory. Everyone wants to make money and a lot of money.

You find out to your surprise for some reason, or another market is not complying with the plan of making a lot of quick cash and is not going in the desired direction. Then all of a sudden it seems that the market is not at all cooperating. Instead, it is going in the wrong direction.

The gut feeling was so clear and compelling when you had entered the trade. It was a sure thing at that time. The business could not go wrong in your opinion. Now it has gone so far in the wrong direction that you may have difficulty in getting out.

Do you know now that most of this evolution of a position gone bad has to do with you entering the market and risking real cash without having a plan, a stop, and a tested money management system before entry? What to do now?

Most of us do not think it painful enough to change our thinking and take sound money management seriously until we suffer a few losing trades to bring the concept home. Now many of us have faced this type of a situation.

What is the psychology of risk control? The psychology of risk control sooner or later begins with genuinely believing that you will benefit from a risk control plan. When you have mastered your psychology, you will experience less anxiety in your business and will be able to implement your business plan more consistently.

So instead of fearing a stop out when your selling system tells you that the trade has gone wrong, think of it as getting a step closer to the winning trade. Never risk more than 2% of your equity on a single business. So if you have a $10,000 buying account, the most you will lose on a single trade will be $200. By limiting your loss potential on each and every trade, you will reduce your level of stress and anxiety during trading.

As you gain confidence in your money management plan, you will begin to see the profits increase. Your pride will grow from generating greater profits from each trade. That increased pride will make you more confident in your abilities to become a successful trader.

Focus on What you Want

The principles and lessons below are necessary to help you move in the direction you wish. It may take some time to implement these entirely, but stick in there and the changes will happen slowly and naturally. Progress is always incrementally one step at a time, so following this pathway will help you to move consistently in the right direction.

1. You Must Focus Consistently On What You Want

You must only and exclusively think of what you want, at the expense of any other thought. This is because where the focus is, is where the energy will begin to flow. By focusing only and directly on what you want at all times, the creative energy can only move to the thing you want. If you are haphazard and always shift between wanting and not wanting something (i.e., the positive and the negative), you ruin the whole focus momentum and energy. It is like going down one road, only to reverse and go back up it constantly over time.

You must move in one direction, and that is the direction of what you want. It may be that this isn't achieved at first, in that some negativity appears. However, stick in there and eventually you will totally focus on what you want at all times. It takes mental training to bring your mind doggedly back to what you want at all times for the real success to be realized.

2. Focus in the Moment

Alongside focusing on what you want, you must keep your mental attention in the present moment. This means the energy is being harnessed, and more access to the subconscious mind can come about. This also allows you to assess any shifts in vibration (i.e., emotional feeling) because the present moment is the most stable mental state.

3. The Key Is To Control the Mind

There are two aspects here. First is to control your focus. The mind should only be in a present moment state. Bring it to this focus every single time and keep it there. The mind will willingly obey over time, and this will be the reality for you. Next, is to focus on what you want. Sometimes we are not doing this without even realizing. We must become conscious of what we are focusing on, and only keep our focus in that one positive direction that allows for success. Positive thinking, feeling, and manifestation should be what we want, and we only put our attention on that.

Training your mind in this way will give enormous dividends over time. Incremental improvement of the level of control will come about, and this will make you the success you desire.

CHAPTER 10

SUCCESSFUL VS AVERAGE PEOPLE

Types of People

I'm going to outline three philosophies that have only harmed humanity and if you're familiar with someone who seems to share a similar ideology as the one described, then you might want to reconsider that relationship...

Hedonists - Hedonism was the dominant philosophy in Ancient Rome, and arguably lead it to its demise. In hedonism, pleasure reigns supreme. These types of people seek out superficial pleasures without giving much thought to the negative effects their actions could potentially cause. The creed of hedonism is "If it feels good, do it!".

This philosophy has been known to produce gluttonous and lustful individuals who consequently have very little determination. Although these people may seem "fun and amusing" at first, you'll soon realize that they won't do you any favors in the long run.

Individualists - An individualist, when faced with a pressing decision will initially think "what can I get out of this?" Individualism is essentially a selfish philosophy that puts the main concern on "you and only you." Individualism servers the community as a whole; these types of people will harm the community to advance themselves. This philosophy is a bit less evident but just as dangerous as the others. It may take you awhile to spot an individualist out but once you do you can either keep your distance or attempt to alter his or her philosophy. Individualists mindset can be changed. However, individualism has proven to be the easiest dogma to alter. A simple wake-up call and some words of wisdom should do the trick.

Minimalists - Minimalism is the rival of greatness and the founder of mediocrity. This philosophy is pretty self-explanatory, "What is the least I can do?" The minimalists want to reap all the rewards while giving none of the efforts. "How can I put forth no effort, but still accomplish everything I want to?" If you spend too much time with these types of people, you'll subconsciously inherit their slothful nature. One thing I have come to realize is that working hard is extremely contagious chose to spend your time with hardworking individuals and the first change you'll notice is your work ethic. Unfortunately, this theory works both ways, spend too much time with a lethargic person, and you'll be at risk for developing a similar work ethic.

Breaking from Average

To be "just" average means you are "just" middle of the road. You are considered normal. The majority of the population is considered average. If you are average than you are among the masses. You are considered common, mainstream, everyday, familiar, regular, and humdrum. Those are a few synonyms that describe the average Joe. I think you get the picture.

Do you consider yourself average? Are you average? I am not sure about you, but I do not want to be just average. I need to be in the above average group.

Everybody's good at something. There is something that you do very well. As a matter of fact, you may be considered above average for the one specific thing you do so well.

My better half is an artist when talking about doing cakes and cupcakes. She is going to do the loveliest cakes, and they taste good too. She just has that extremely special talent that is far above the average person, when it boils down to decorating cakes. Her phone never stops ringing. She's above average when it boils down to cakes.

What puts somebody into the above average category? What are some examples or prerequisites that may take you there?

First, there has to be the want too. Why do you want to be a successful network marketer? Is it the money? The ability to meet new people? Do you like traveling around the country? This is going to be a very important factor in deciding if you are average or above average.

How is your drive? How motivated are you? How much did Michael Jordan wish to play basketball for his high school team after he did not make the cut? He said that he was devastated. He started working and working hard. His heart was to play basketball. The following step was to work harder than anyone else did. Everyone knows what all that tough work did for Michael Jordan.

When I played sports, I wanted to be the best I could be. I didn't want to let my teammates down. I would be in the gym working out on the bench press. I was struggling to get the last push I had in me. I was ready to give up when a friend of mine came up to spot me. He yelled, "Gosur you aren't ready to quit. You've got two more in you. Let's Go!" He would encourage me, and before I was done, I would do three, four, or five more.

You see, I had a mental block in me that said I could only do so much. When I reached that line, I was done. When my friend came to help me out, he pushed me beyond that line that I thought I couldn't go. That's the line that separates success from failure.

Will you fail? Yes, you will. Will you quit? NEVER! It needs effort, endurance, and the will that says; I'll never give up until I reach my goal. I'm going to be ready never to give up until I cross over that line to my success.

Line up with mentors, and individuals that work diligently, that will inspire and challenge you across that finish line. You're the average of the 5 folks you spend the most time with. So choose your associates well.

Want to be above average?

1. Find out your why.
2. Than find out how bad do you want it.
3. Than line up with good mentors and leaders 4. Last, roll up your sleeves and get to work.

Success or average? It's your decision.

Overcoming Fear of Failure and Ridicule

No one gets to the finish line successfully without passing through the roads of failure. This holds true for many people if not the entire human race. You may refer to the encyclopedia to know the names of people who have failed more than a hundred times before achieving success in their field. It is neither their money nor their charm that helped them gain victory but their ability to overcome the fear of failure.

If you were wondering where they take their strength from, they would probably answer, 'experience' which you may be trying to avoid. Failure is a larger than life experience that makes or breaks, the reason why you fear it. Some people choose to pull off the road, and others keep their hopes up and continue the journey. You may not always see failure coming, but the best part is that you tried. You must know too that failure never wins for a determined individual. Like ghosts, they become more empowered when they smell fear.

To overcome fear of failure, careful planning and emotional, physical and financial preparation, is required. In meeting life's biggest challenges, your mind, body, and soul should be in tune. Mental and emotional health paves the way to positive ideas. Below are additional suggestions on how you can overcome these negative feelings:

Fear of failure is your enemy that you must know well. When you know how it works, you will know how to fight it. But first be ready to face failure once it stared you in the face.

Consider taking the risk. As you may be aware of, there is no guarantee that you will succeed on the first try that is why it is called 'risk.' Remember that when you take the risk, you welcome all the possibilities.

Think about the opportunities and lessons that you will miss when you remain fearful of failure. If you want to be an entrepreneur, you must be financially and emotionally prepared so that when it did not work out, you still have a fallback.

Anticipate failure. In anything you do, expect that at one point or another, failure will or may happen. Being prepared for it lessens the burden and even boosts your confidence. Try looking at different areas of your undertaking and turn it upside down before you go. As soon as you have conditioned your mind to this fact of life, you can now move to the next step.

There are many different ways on how to overcome fear of failure but keep in mind that these would not work to your advantage if you refuse to cooperate. Sometimes, you have no options but to accept it. While you think you have everything well planned out, you lose your track and get lost in a dilemma. These worse-case scenarios are what you should be prepared for.

Should you need further help or to be inspired, get help from books and encouraging quotations. These somehow ease your anxiety and remind you of the possibilities that failure is just waiting around the corner as well as success. Acknowledge that both will be present in your journey. The most important thing to come from you first is the strength to overcome fear of failure and success will come to you as strongly as the failure did. Failure has always been the price of success which if you are not willing to pay, would collect interest until you lost the enthusiasm to move on.

CHAPTER 11

WHAT MAKES BILLIONAIRES DIFFERENT

It is not easy to become rich in this competitive world, where earning money is a difficult task. To be successful as the individuals who have turned into billionaires in this competitive environment, you should try to develop a mindset similar to those who have succeeded at it in the past, and get to know the various secrets which are associated with it.

Remain positive. If you have a positive attitude to life, despite all the failures that come your way, it is quite possible to achieve what you want and become wealthy in the process.

Follow your passion and commit to it fully. This helps if you enjoy what you do and provide you with rich dividends when you emerge successfully. Your hard work tends to pay off at some point in time, and this certainly proves that you have managed to emerge successful, despite all the odds.

When you want to get rich through a Billionaire Mindset, it is advisable that you keep up with the latest financial buzz and the people who create this buzz, because you could just find your path to your riches with the help of this knowledge.

The generation of an idea depends on upon the way you think. The person who thinks big has the tendency to generate big and innovative ideas comparing to other people. The person must have courage and ability to hold on to the big idea to be able to achieve big things. There are failures in the people's life who think big, but the major point is to hold on to a vision. Failure helps you to learn and brings better ways to achieve your goals.

Have the courage to think big is to find what you love. The people no interest in a particular subject lack creative ideas for their goals. After you find your subject of interest, study about the life of the great people who have achieved big things in the particular subject which will provide you confidence to achieve big things in that subject.

When you suffer from the failure in trying something new, just remember the life of great people who have failed many times before they have achieved big things in their life, this will encourage you to hold on and learn from your failure Your curiosity and passion will help you to achieve big things in your life which are the reason you must have the courage to hold on and learn. Curiosity will help you to explore new and innovative ideas which will help you to achieve bigger things in life. Always remember that each and every great thing were new at some point in time and those achievements are the result of having a big vision.

While there are bricks and stones that build houses, our characters are the one building for our success or failure. No matter how many books or seminars have we attended about successful entrepreneurship and relationship if we lack the characters that speak to these things, we can't possibly move from were we are at the moment. Values about life are the one that will teach us of characters for the successful relationship with people who will be our tool towards building successful and rewarding careers.

Humility

Be humble like a duck-but it doesn't mean you have to be timid and silent to be humble. Being passive is different from being humble. Humility is a character that listens instead of monopolizing the talk. Humility is about appreciation of other people's success to look upon them instead of mocking them. Being humble is accepting the limits of things and failures to find more opportunities. And humility is about taking the past defeats and loses as lessons in life instead of condemning and regretting everything. And all people are born with this character. But as we go to the world and experience bad things, we build arrogance and conceit to hide the ugliness of our past. And instead of achieving the things we wanted, we always fail. If all people are humble enough, then the war would have not occurred.

Perseverance

It's difficult to persevere if every plan we have goes awry. That's why few people achieve the success in life they wanted. Perseverance is a man's drive to continue despite the odds and difficulties in life. Innovations in Technologies, Inventions, empires, kingdoms, etc. were built due to a man's perseverance to succeed. Sticking to the fight and unmindful of the odds are what wins a player. Many people have the tendency to lose perseverance especially if they go out beyond their comfort zone. Being in the midst of crisis is a sign that you tried and persevered because you went beyond your limits. And if you get out from that crisis it means you have succeeded and win the fight.

Optimism

The easiest character to build is optimism because it gives us hope and light. When we think of good things, goals and plans in life we are building optimism in our life. Optimism helps us grow as a person because we plan and we set goals to achieve this. But when we are hit with bad events and failures it's easy also to let go of this character. Negative thoughts enter our mind and we began to lose hope. We know how to control our mind, and it's easy to rebuild our dreams again. Living life with optimism means you choose happiness and hope as your setting goal in your life.

CHAPTER 12

THE ECONOMICALLY PRODUCTIVE HOUSEHOLD

Having and economically productive household is something that's not entirely new. However, because of technology, it has become easier for both employer and employee to work together even if both are located miles away from each other. This is why more and more companies are allowing their employees to work from home. However, you don't have to be an employee to enjoy the benefits of telecommuting. There are many other ways to earn at home, and we will explore some of them in this chapter.

Micro-jobs

One of the most popular ways to earn money at home now is through websites that offer micro-jobs. The jobs offered on these websites can be done in as little as 10 minutes, and once you finish, your work will be checked, and you will get paid. In most cases, workers can simply apply for the job by bidding and if chosen, the worker is usually given a deadline to finish the job and once submitted, the worker is compensated through their payment preference.

Technical Work at Home Jobs

All work at home jobs requires both an internet connection and a computer, so you need to have at least basic working knowledge of technology. This alone can already help you earn money. Knowing the basics of social media and a few marketing skills can get you a job as a promoter. Also, if you have advanced skills in computers, you can also work as a website developer or a technical support representative. These jobs don't require an office so skills in these areas can get you work at home job.

Creative Work at Home Jobs

If you are not exactly a technical person, a little knowledge in computers and a lot of creativity can also get you work at home job. There are many writing jobs out there that are being outsourced so if you are capable of writing great quality articles, you can find work that you can do at home. Also, graphic artists are in demand now in work at home industry, and if you have the skills and reliable equipment, you can also consider becoming one.

Beginning a home business is among the most rewarding times imaginable. You will give yourself the freedom of working from your home and will have the flexibility to plan your schedule. The piece that follows offers several useful ideas for ensuring that your home business enterprise is a success.

CHAPTER 13

SAVING HABITS OF BILLIONAIRES

There are several habits that when once develop, saving becomes your culture.

1. Decide To Save - decide to start saving money. The basic rule is 10% of your income. Get a bookkeeper or personal financial software and start tracking your expenses. Find out where your money is going. Your home based business has tax advantages that can help you save more.
2. Make your savings an expense - Pay yourself first. Treat your savings like your car note, credit card bill, or mortgage payment. Most people cringe when bill collectors call. Use that same fear to save. Have automatic deductions from your checking account, paycheck, or merchant account go right into your savings. Just like taxes are taking out of a paycheck and most people don't notice it. You won't notice the automatic deductions.
3. Read for 15-30 minutes per day - Your home based business depends on you. Leaders are readers. Read books on

personal finance, money management, investing, and personal development. Start with the Richest Man in Babylon, by George Clauson, followed by Think and Grow Rich, by Napoleon Hill.

4. Pay off your debts - Some experts say that you should pay off your debts first. From my experience, I say do both. I remember paying off all my debts and still did not have money saved. When I went back into debt when unexpected expenses arrived. Put a portion of your income to savings and a portion of the debt.

Develop a habit of saving money now. Your home based business depends on it. A habit of saving money is the best way to take care of emergencies, unexpected expenses, and it gives you the ability to act when business opportunities arrive.

Cultivating Saving Habit

Saving money is the art of setting aside some amount of money for future use. The singular reason why so many people don't always get enough money to do what they want or need is that they don't have a good saving habit. In this section, you will learn 6 effective ways to help you start saving money.

1. Determine what you want:

It is very important that you determine what you want to do with money and the time when you would want to use it. Doing this will help ascertain what you should set aside and over what period, for instance, if you desire to save $5,000 within six months, you should be saving about $830 every month. This amount can also be broken down into weeks or days depending on your convenience. What matters most is to ensure that you have a time frame for which to accomplish your goal.

2. Map Out a Plan:

Having established what you want to do with the money you intend to save and over a period, your next task will be to come up with a plan of how you intend to go about the saving. Your plan should entail where to save the money, do you need interests, how often you should save, etc. Planning will help you reach your goal much easier and it will take care of any unforeseen hitches on the way.

3. Discipline:

One of the major reason why lots of people fail to cultivate the habit of saving money is that they lack the discipline required to effective pull through with the plan of saving. Discipline helps you stay focused and committed to your plan. Once you have a plan in place to save some money over a period, you need the discipline to see you through it. Some distractions may come up along the way, but discipline will enable you to pull through.

4. Sacrifice:

Saving demands that you forgo some regular spending routine, the truth is that once you have made up your mind to start saving some money, you will have to make some sacrifices to provide for your savings. By sacrificing some leisure, it means you are making some money available to save. In this case, you will have to differentiate between your needs and wants. One of the best ways to save money is to avoid spending on things you don't need. Besides, when you sacrifice, you should also have it at the back of your mind that it is a temporal basis. That is why it is important that you have a time frame for your saving.

5. Carry Everyone Along:

In the course of saving money, there are so many things that will change with you, especially if you have a family or dependent. In this case, you should endeavor to carry your family and any other person who depends on you financially along. You should be able to communicate your goal to them, am sure if you are convincing enough, they will reason with you.

Saving money is the most effective way to become wealthy in life, no wonder only those who cultivate the habit of saving money can survive in today's economy.

Reasons for Saving

Do you remember the old saying "save for the rainy day"? Can you recall the fable of the ant and the grasshopper we learned when we were young which taught us to save money? Of course, we remember those lessons, yet we don't practice them. It is true that saving money is the greatest secret to building wealth. For you to meet financial security and financial freedom, you need to have a good amount of savings. You are lucky if you are part of the rich clans and have a huge inheritance from your parents' wealth. But what if your parents decided to give it all to charities? Then you're left with nothing. Whether you wanted to become rich or not, you still need to save money.

Here are four important reasons why you still need to save money no matter what:

1. Survive financial crises. This is in the form of accident, illness, job loss, failure of business, or sudden death either you or one of your family members. Whether this is an act of God or act of nature, there are huge financial losses and we need money to survive. We may find a short-term solution to these problems, but we might end up having huge sums of debts. Adequate savings will give you peace of mind that you can survive any emergency that comes your way.
2. Improve the life and well-being of your family. They said that money cannot buy happiness, but it can certainly buy things that will uplift our quality of life and our families. Sufficient savings can help us buy a decent house, a car, pay for quality education or to start-up business. It can also give simple pleasures for your love ones like treating them to vacations or trips. It can also strengthen married life. Most couples argue about the lack of money. With enough savings, we can avoid disagreements about finances.
3. Enjoy your retirement.
4. Economic development.

Whether you wanted to become rich or not, you still need to save money. Believe it or not, money makes the world go round. Money is essential for our survival and in this world and age, things are no longer free. To secure your future, you need to save money and start early so you can enjoy its fruits sooner.

CHAPTER 14

FIND A WAY TO INCREASE YOUR INCOME

When the economy is in a downturn naturally many people are looking for ways to both save money, and where possible to increase their income.

The obvious things to look at are in the areas of employment. With your job, can you seek a promotion to a different level which will mean an increase in salary? Do you have skills which might help you find a part-time job to supplement your wage, even if only as a temporary measure? It might mean working for a few hours in the evening after your normal job has finished. It could be something that you can do on the Internet if you can find a niche. There are various ways to increase your income if you have the initiative. That bit of extra income could just be enough to get you by until some of your debts are paid off.

If married, there could be other ways to increase your income. Could your partner find a job for themselves, even if only part-time? It's surprising how often just a small but regular wage can make a big difference to the family finances. People of working age who are still living at home should be expected to contribute towards the costs of running a home, so work out a realistic amount for them to hand over.

If, unfortunately, you are out of work, as so many are in this economic climate, what steps are you taking to look for work? Someone once said that getting a job is a job in itself. That is so true. There are so many people often all applying for the same position that employers can pick and choose the best. You need to stand out from the crowd. Don't just rely on the jobcentre, but put your CV on sites where you can register with job agencies, though you need to make sure the agency is reputable. Nowadays there is little excuse for not having a well-written CV. There is a range of templates which take you through step by step showing you how to fill in a CV. Send off letters on spec to employers you think might be hiring. If you are interested, say, in retail work, call in some stores on the off chance they are looking for staff. Above all, try to stay positive.

Hopefully, some of the above suggestions about ways to increase your income may be of help in giving you freedom from debt.

Even if you are on a good salary, with the expenses rising every day, all of us require sorting out an extra income to ensure that not only can they get hold of the money required to meet their daily requirements, they can also save some money towards a more secure future. While there are some options to consider with seeing an extra income coming towards you each month, let us look at some of the safest options.

The Internet and Online Money Making

If you are already working and have a fixed job to cater to, you will probably be able to offer only a couple of hours every day to increase your income. Under such circumstances, the internet can be a great way to go for this extra bit of money. There are a huge number of business opportunities that you will come across over the internet.

Consider options like affiliate marketing, forex trading, stocks, and so on. While affiliate marketing and other such campaigns (like Pay Per Click advertising) can show you good money and yet lesser risks, stocks and forex trading can be quite risky and requires you to be an expert on the subject. If you are not very knowledgeable on these options, it is a good idea to consider educating yourself on them before trying them out.

The Right Research

Affiliate marketing can show you good results as well, but it might take some time before you can see good money coming in from it to increase your income. And if you are wondering about the stocks and forex, it can be a good idea to get in touch with a good financial investment company, work with them closely, and learn the trades from them before you plan on going solo.

These were some of the immediate ways, or short term ways, to make money. However, if you are planning on improving your financial condition on a long term basis, there are a good number of investment plans that you can always check out! These schemes can offer you great returns, helping your money grow with time. Some of these investment plans are very safe, and can even work towards an annuity.

For this, you need to sort out a few things. How much money can you invest every month after setting aside money for your expenses, and also some money for liquid savings? When would you want to see the returns coming towards you? How safe is the plan you are opting for? Will it improve your credit score?

And there are some other questions that you should consider. Get in touch with a good finance company to understand your options with regards to how to increase your income in the best possible way, starting today!

Attitude to Possess

There are commonly held attitudes that interfere with the ability to increase your income. Sometimes, you're aware of having these attitudes and where they come from. Often though you have no awareness of them and that is when they are particularly deadly. Then, they are unseen obstacles. You don't even understand what the problem is. Let's look at a few of the most common attitudes that get in the way of clients when they want to increase their income. Do you have some of these attitudes?

1) I don't care about money.

If you have the belief that you don't care about money, you're either poor or lying to yourself. You may have the image that is caring about making money also means that you are greedy, ruthless, or willing to do anything for money. These images cause you to limit your efforts to increase your income. Yes, these may sometimes seem to be truisms. However, believing a character limits you. Money gives you greater freedom and more latitude to contribute positively in the world. Keep your virtues intact and simply be a good businessperson when pursuing increased income.

2) I want to get rich overnight without any work.

This childlike fantasy can set you up for every "get rich quick" scheme in existence. You're better off to think of increasing your income as a long-term or medium-term project and to accept the fact that it takes a lot of hard work. What's so great about avoiding hard work anyway? You're working for yourself to improve the financial conditions of your life. Isn't that enough motivation to get you working? You might want to change this attitude into being cautious about any claims that you can get rich overnight without any investment of hard work.

3) It's not "spiritual" or ethical to want to increase my income.

There's an attitude-which might come from religious indoctrination-that you would lose your soul if you seek to gain financially. What gets lost in this attitude is that these spiritual teachings also state that it is the pursuit of money that is the problem- meaning that pursuit above all else that is the problem.

The loss of any spiritual foundation isn't necessarily implied by increasing your income. It's not mutually exclusive that pursuing increasing your income means you can't keep your spiritual and ethical foundation intact. In fact, having both is extremely powerful and can be a wonderful contributor to the world.

4) If I just do what I love, the money will come to me.

Yes, it is important that you focus on doing what you love and love what you are doing while working to increase your income. You must be realistic also though. This is a fine fantasy, but without the foundation of business, you could spend a lot of time, energy, and money pursuing a plan that has no potential for increasing your income. You need to ask yourself things like:

- Is there a demand for what I want to do?
- Do people willingly spend money on what I want to sell?
- Do I have business skills?
- Do I know how to turn this love into a money-making enterprise?
- Am I willing to do what it takes to turn it into a money-making enterprise?

5) I don't have to take care of the money I get. Somehow that's a "dirty" activity.

Another attitude that can get in your way is the refusal to manage the money that you do have. If you don't manage your existing money, why do you think you'd be able to manage your increased income? Managing your money and accounting for its income and outgo builds respect for the fruits of your labor. It is a self-respecting attitude. Cultivate careful money management and investment of your surplus and your chances of increasing your income radically improve.

These are just a few of the attitudes that are most prevalent and the biggest obstacles to increase your income. Just because you have learned these attitudes and let them "run" you doesn't mean that you must continue that behavior. You can change your beliefs. You can take new attitudes. You can eliminate these self-imposed obstacles.

Limit Borrowing

Every time you borrow money, it is best to carefully consider if doing such is the right decision. Borrowing money means you're in a commitment to repay it back within the given time frame. How borrowing such amount would affect your future finances is something you should consider. It will be smart to ask yourself these questions before borrowing.

Do I Need to Purchase This Now?

Most of the time, the things that seem necessary aren't. You can delay or postpone the purchases until you have enough money to buy the item. Doing the laundry yourself might help you save much money for you. If it is just for recreational activities such as jet skis or long boards, you can let it go by for now and save the money, because they are less necessary purchases. In fact, it will help you save up more money than expected because you will be more motivated to make the purchases.

Can I Purchase Something That's Less Expensive Instead?

When making big purchases, you always want to get the nicest of what you can afford. However, you can get pretty much the same results by getting a close look at how much is needed. For instance, if you plan on purchasing a car, you may consider spending three to five thousand on the car instead of seven to ten thousand. With a smaller amount, you can still find a reliable and decent car for less, and you save yourself an amount which you can use towards saving or investing in your fu future.

Can I Afford to Make the Payments?

This is probably the most important question to answer in full honestly. How this purchase will affect your ability to do things in the future is something you should highly consider. It may mean you need to take fewer vacations because you don't have the ability to save much money. Additionally, you may be very tight with that budget that it is making it difficult for you to do anything. You may come to regret the purchase, and wish that you could turn back the time to change your decision.

How Fast Can I Pay It Off?

When taking out a loan, you should focus and have a plan for repaying the loan as quickly as possible. It is essential to realize that building true wealth is more difficult when you are regularly paying interest to others. Turning this around and can help you earn money with your money, you'll be able to reach your financial goals. That is why carefully considering all your options before you borrow money is very important.

What Happens If I Can't Pay It Off?

You should also think about the long-term effects of losing your job is something that is possible to happen. This means that there will be extra pressure on your part to find a new job quickly because any delayed or skipped payments will affect your credit score. Depending on the industry you are currently in, finding another job might be difficult if you have a poor credit history. You need to consider and look for options on how you can pay this loan off should you lose your job.

CHAPTER 15

ROADBLOCKS

It's true, in the beginning when your starting out, it's the hardest time to get ahead. This is the #1 reason why so few people become Billionaires, because they lack the persistence to get over the "hump" where you start to have things working in your favor. It's important to realize that becoming a billionaire and building wealth include both the ability to impress wealth on your subconscious mind as well as learn the skills of the marketplace.

1. Develop an Internal Belief System of You as Wealthy
2. Know How of Wealth Building, Financial Plans, Through Leveraged Accumulation
3. Make your Move, The Most Critical Step!

How do you precisely become a billionaire? Comply with these:

1. They live within their suggests.

Sure, they have big houses and possibly quite a few vehicles. Nevertheless, they may well be within the similar building for the past several years. Warren Buffet still lives inside the same house for far more than 30 years. A range drive second-hand automobiles or send their children to widespread schools. They dress in suits only when they are meeting clients. Otherwise, you'll be able to hardly tell they're basically billionaires.

2. They stick to a budget.

See, they don't splurge their hard-earned money at all. After all, they understand the value of hard work and determination. Additionally they possess a lot of men and women to take care of. Thus, to produce positive they can meet their needs and wants without going overboard, they do create their own spending budget, possibly with the assist of their accountants.

3. They continue being beneficial.

Majority of these self-made billionaires have met a great deal of challenges along the way. They too experienced failures. Even so, they have remained good and didn't allow such things to ruin their self-confidence.

Some do make use of subliminal messages or affirmations. These are the men and women who know the power of subliminal messages specifically when you are talking about changing your very own perception on issues. Subliminal messages can assist you stay beneficial despite the troubles. Good examples include the following:

- I can surely beat these difficulties.
- I will not permit challenges to pull me down.

- I know that when you are down, there's nowhere to go but up.
- I have the self-assurance and skill to create it big someday.

4. They delegate duties.

They know how you can stick to the Pareto principle or the 80-20 rule. Not a great deal of people today are aware that only 20 percent of their duties can possess a huge impact; the rest really don't. For those the details that truly matter, they take command, but they distribute the 80 percent menial tasks to the employees. This way, they have a lot more time for the bigger fish.

They also do not micromanage. This signifies they don't always spend a lot of time checking every single detail of other people's perform. They hire competent managers to do just that. They also care for their men and women too, knowing that the greatest resource will likely be the company's men and women.

5. They invest their funds.

They don't just maintain their hard-earned money within the banks, where they earn quite little interest. They do invest. They acquire stocks and bonds, opt for mutual funds, or place a little amount for insurance and pensions. They diversify their portfolio to guarantee not all their cash disappear just in case the economy doesn't turn out to be great.

CONCLUSION

Do you want an extraordinary, wealthy lifestyle?

Creating wealth requires you to learn a set of skills, and to think a certain way.

Only 1-3% of people become wealthy because they take the time to learn the skills and strategies to create wealth, and they are willing to do what it takes to succeed.

Secret 1:

You need to truly value wealth to get it! Everyone can become a billionaire in direct proportion to their value system. This simply means that we are inspired to do things that are high on our list of values, but we delay and procrastinate when it comes to the things that are low on our list of values, because they are not a big priority in our lives or we are uncomfortable with them

Donald Trump had read every book on property and wealth he could get his hands on by the time he was 11 years old. He was determined to learn the skills and create wealth in his life.

If you are truly committed to wealth building, you need to start on the journey now. At the very least you need to be saving more than spending and investing to increase your assets.

It is not how much money you make but how you manage what you make that creates wealth.

Secret 2:

Whoever has the most certainty creates the most wealth. You need to start from a measurable grounded position. Most people live in a fantasy world when it comes to creating wealth; the facts are all very nebulous. They don't know where their starting point is in real figures, and they don't know where they are going in real figures. They have a 'story' in their mind that they will be wealthy one day but have no plan or strategy to get there (wherever 'there' is!).

If you say you want a lifestyle of financial independence, what does that mean to you? What does it look like? How much do you need in real figures? Have you factored in inflation? What is your strategy for getting there? How much do you have to save every month? Is it doable? You need to start from a doable position and then accelerate it as your wealth builds?

GETTING GROUNDED IS ESSENTIAL!!

Wealthy people keep detailed information about every asset they have - value, insurance, history - and continually update it. They know exactly where they are!

Wealth building is a measurable, ongoing journey of learning. It has a known starting point, a methodical plan or map, and a specific destination.

As you start on the journey, as you learn the skills and become a master through doing it day after day, your goals will get bigger and bigger. You will find it easy to amass more and more wealth.

First, take the time to put everything down on paper in detail:

- The value of each of your current assets if you were to sell them.
- Your lifestyle goals and how long will it take you to get there?
- The strategies you will use to get there.
- What income per year will you need?
- How can you increase savings? How can you increase income?
- What passive streams of income will you implement?

Secret 3:

Your wealth building needs to have a BIG WHY! Linking your pursuit of wealth to a cause that will transform the world in some way will empower you and keep the dream alive. You can't get beyond your fears if you don't have a big enough reason.

The greater your cause, the greater your wealth potential.

Everybody wants to do something amazing with their lives, something that inspires them. They don't have to motivate themselves to do it because it is a passion. It is something that brings tears to their eyes.

Richard Branson invited some of the wealthiest businessmen on the planet to his island to brainstorm ideas for businesses that could be set up to solve some of the world's greatest problems. They each paid him $100, 000 for the privilege of being there, for being part of a meaningful cause.

If you live to your higher values, you will do greater things in life than you normally would. There is nothing more inspiring than seeing someone discover what their values are and using them to serve others.

Most of us live our lives with paradigms that are not even ours, and that is even incongruent with our value system. We subordinate our true selves. Find your uniqueness, your values and needs and honor yourself. Manifestation comes from 'knowing thyself'.

You want to be able to go to bed at night saying with tears in your eyes, "thank you for who I am and what I can do to serve others."

Build wealth from integrated well-being!

Thank you for taking time in reading this book. I believe it has been an amazing experience walk-through of billionaires' lifestyle.

CONGRATULATIONS!!

YOU have finished reading this book. I as the author hope you really enjoyed this book. Remember please don't forget to leave me a 5-star review. If you don't think i deserve a 5-star review, please just don't leave one and rather send me an email so i can make this book a 5-star book at cbashsuperdome@gmail.com.

Also, Checkout my other 5-star books:

Financial Planning and Debt Planning: How to Plan a Successful Life

https://www.amazon.com/Financial-Planning-Debt-Plan-Successful-ebook/dp/B077LF3YV2

The Awesome Power of Social Media: How Social Media has Changed Everything

https://www.amazon.com/Awesome-Power-Social-Media-Everything-ebook/dp/B079CL449X

The Power of Perseverance: Proven Steps and Strategies of Achieving Success Through Perseverance

https://www.amazon.com/Power-Perseverance-Strategies-Achieving-Success-ebook/dp/B078WLFBZN

Checkout and Reach me at:

Facebook.com/wisebookz

Twitter.com/cbashsuperdome

www.ingramcontent.com/pod-product-compliance
Lightning Source LLC
Chambersburg PA
CBHW052154220526
45471CB00004B/1675